Divorce and the Children

H.S. Vigeveno and Anne Claire

GL Regal Books

A Division of G/L Publications
Glendale, California, U.S.A.

Other good Regal reading by H.S. Vigeveno
Dear David
Jesus the Revolutionary
13 Men Who Changed the World

The foreign language publishing of all Regal books is under the direction of *Gospel Literature International* (GLINT), a missionary assistance organization founded in 1961 by Dr. Henrietta C. Mears. Each year *Gospel Literature International* provides financial and technical help for the adaptation, translation and publishing of books and Bible study materials in more than 85 languages for millions of people worldwide.

For more information you are invited to write *Gospel Literature International*, Glendale, California 91204.

Scripture quotations in this publication are from the following versions:
Phillips, The New Testament in Modern English, Revised Edition, J.B. Phillips, Translator. © J.B. Phillips 1958, 1960, 1972. Used by permission of Macmillan Publishing Co., Inc.
RSV, From the RSV of the Bible, copyrighted 1946 and 1952 by the Division of Christian Education of the NCCC, U.S.A., and used by permission.
AMP, Amplified Bible, The. Copyright © 1962, 1964 by Zondervan Publishing House. Used by permission.
NASB, New American Standard Bible. © The Lockman Foundation 1960, 1962, 1963, 1968, 1971. Used by permission.

Published by Regal Books Division, G/L Publications
Glendale, California 91209
Printed in U.S.A.

Library of Congress Catalog Card No. 78-067855
ISBN 0-8307-0645-3

In grateful appreciation
to the many children and parents
who made this book possible.
We thank you for sharing your lives
in order to help others.

Contents

Introduction

Is Divorce Tough on Children?

"Our home was a battleground. No place to raise children. Everybody's better off now that we're divorced."

"Tommy's too young to understand. Someday he'll learn to accept the fact that his parents did what they thought best."

"Of course I'm concerned about my children. But I'm also concerned about me, about my happiness. Kids are resilient; they'll bounce back."

Sound familiar? Perhaps you said something like this when you divorced. The "everything-will-work-out-the-children-will-be-fine" philosophy is definitely part of the divorce picture today. But is it realistic? In our research we talked to children of divorced families from diversified social and economic backgrounds. Was divorce destructive to them? Were they disturbed, unsettled or troubled? For how long?

"Mom and Dad don't care about me. All they think

7

of is themselves," 10-year-old Heather tearfully said. "Sometimes I feel like running away."

Fifteen-year-old Johnny's parents were recently divorced. He says, "If Dad brings his girlfriend to my baseball game I'm just going to ignore them. How can I explain about them to the other guys?"

"I often wish for my real dad, that we were together. On family shows on TV I see that bond between the father, the mother and the children. I often wish I had that."

"I asked Mommy, 'Why did you and Daddy get divorced?' I asked her lots of times. She said that everyone would be happier this way. She said we would be unhappy children if we stayed together. Sometimes I cry."

"It *was* and *is the most traumatic thing* that ever happened in my life: It completely changed everything. This divorce really shook me up. It just kept me at 13 emotionally until I was 20."

Yes, divorce is tough on children. It was a popular theory a few years ago for couples with children to say: "We will stay together until they are 21, and then good-bye marriage!" Today divorce is occurring at an alarming, increasing rate—even among Christian families—regardless of the ages of the children. Religious leaders are concerned; educators are concerned; psychologists are concerned; and most parents are concerned. They fear the effects of divorce on children.

We are concerned. We have written this book to show how children are affected and how you can help them and yourself through the trauma of a family break-up.

The voices of the children come from all over the United States. Each child responded differently as no two children grow and develop at the same rate. Each child had a unique reaction to the tearing apart of a family. Some children were not even able to verbalize their feelings because the experience was too new. Some children were able to work their way out because of special help: "This divorce helped me to cope better. I have had to rely on God more, rather than a happy family life. It's helped me to grow. It's just a trial you have to conquer."

Read the children's stories and hear what they are saying. Discover what you can do to help them as you see divorce from their viewpoint. We believe we have found some answers and this book can help you.

H. S. Vigeveno

Anne Claire

Part I

Dealing with Divorce

1

What Does Divorce Really Do to the Kids?

At what age does divorce first make an impact on the children involved? Many parents believe a young child is not aware of problems they may be having in their marriage. They thank God that their children are "too young to remember."

Children talked openly with us about their parents' divorce. As they looked back on the time when the divorce happened they provided helpful insights on how it affected them at that particular age in their lives. Indeed, we discovered that the age of a child when the divorce occurs plays a dominant role in how he or she copes with the conflicts and emotions present.

"Maybe Daddy Left Because I'm Not a Boy"

How much does an infant sense, realize, accept or express in the first two years of its life? Divorced parents may not believe that their infants are affected since the small children probably will not show it on the surface. But who can measure the loss of security for an infant?

Angela was only a year old when her parents divorced. Now she is a precocious eight-year-old and lives with her mother. Her father has remarried and Angela has an older stepsister. How did Angela show her loss of security after her parents divorced?

"Mom says that when I was about two or three I sometimes would burst into tears. Suddenly, and I'd say, 'I want my daddy.' But I don't remember that too well. I used to think the divorce was my fault because Daddy kept saying I was supposed to be a boy! But I couldn't help being a girl. If my mother and father would get divorced now, when I'm eight, I'd probably say, 'I'm to blame.' But a child is not to blame for what the parents do. I mean, what the parents do is their choice! It's like you are you, and your mom is your mom and your dad is your dad. I don't blame my mother and I don't blame my dad either. It's like if you try to put a key into a lock and the key is the wrong one. It isn't going to fit. Same thing with a marriage. If you got one person that is different from another, the key just doesn't fit. And then it's best not to keep going. But some people fight it, and that's worse. But you're only human."

Angela's unusual intelligence has helped her to think creatively with a great deal of maturity. Children have fears and frightening dreams. Often they believe they are the cause of their parents' divorce. But Angela has already worked her way through that. However, many children are not able to shake off this sense of guilt as easily as she has. They carry it with them into adulthood and often seek counseling as a result of these early experiences.

What other problems does Angela have as she is adjusting to a home without a father?

"Now and then I really want to visit my dad. I see him about once a year. Sometimes I stay overnight. Sometimes I only stay for the day. Sometimes Gail [her father's wife] is out of the house or something and it's just me and Daddy. So we get some time together."

Does Angela have any problems in school?

"In school what happens is the kids are too young to know about this stuff. Or they're old enough to know that it really isn't a problem. There's nothing wrong with being divorced. At six or seven they usually understand. They don't bug you with it. The fours and fives they don't know."

What would Angela tell a friend whose parents were divorcing?

"Well. The first thing I would do is to sit down and think for a couple of minutes. Then, I'd probably say, *it takes a little while to adjust.* Having the family fall apart is kind of a big thing. And some kids are very sensitive like I am, but I took the divorce pretty well. Anyway, the real sensitive kids don't respond to that very good. I would tell them that they will understand. It just takes a little while to adjust."

Does Angela get angry?

"Sometimes I get angry at Mom. Oh, yeah! Like she doesn't understand things, and then I get all upset. I try to explain and she says, 'I already know what you're talking about.' And like she ignores me. Then I wish that Daddy was here. When you split up, you know, it's kind of like when you have a leg chopped off. Like you're missing something. You feel empty right there. Well, it's like a family. You're missing a person. That's even a bigger thing!"

Does Angela want her mother to marry again?

"I'd be so happy. But I'd worry about the kind of man she would marry. Friends aren't always true. You got to really be with him for a couple of years until you actually know. Some of those teenage kids when they go out they

13

think in a split second, 'Oh we gotta get married.' Well, it's not that way. You might make a wrong move. I'm going to wait till I'm 27 or 29 or 30."

(Her mother would like a copy of this interview on tape when Angela turns 20.)

"Daddy Showed Me Pictures of His Children, and I Cried"

A child between the ages of three to seven usually has no idea what is taking place during a divorce and cannot be expected to comprehend too much. But once he is drawn into the conflict he can be severely impressed. When the divorce is final he realizes that his home is broken and so is his security. Sometimes it takes many years for a child to recover from his resentment.

Gwen is now 18 but she remembers the trauma of her younger years. "My mom won out getting the children, but there were fights about that. I was separated from my father for a long time. I resent my father. It was at least five years before I was told that he had remarried. Even then I didn't realize that he had left my mother for that lady. He showed me pictures of his children, and that hurt me. I cried.

"And now he's married *again* and this wife has three children and they have one of their own. I don't like to feel I'm part of their family. I'm just not."

Ava is also 18. She was 3 when her parents divorced. "My dad took me to Europe for a year and my mom didn't know where I was. Mom finally found me and there was a total battle. I remember the phone calls and she'd hold the receiver out and I could hear my dad screaming back. Slamming doors and high voices! And then it settled down. Now I go to see him when I want to. My mom and dad are not good friends, but it's kind of calmed down.

14

"When I lived with my mom she spoke against my dad all the time. Everything was negative. I always sided with my mom until this past summer. My dad asked me to put flowers on his mom's grave when I went to Europe. And I sat there for an hour and I talked with the Lord at the grave, and I asked Him to put love in my heart, because I don't love my dad. Since then I've really tried, and it's made an improvement. My dad has no faith at all. He's got to a point where he says, 'God bless you,' and that's a big step forward! When I tell him I'm going to a Bible study, he says, 'I'm glad you've got religion. You didn't get it from me.' That's true! My mom and stepdad just became Christians and that's really special."

Larry was 5 and Gretchen 3 when their parents separated. Neither child remembers too much because their mother attempted to shield them from reality. Now Larry is 10 and Gretchen 8.

"I felt kind of bad. I asked Mommy later, 'Why did you and Daddy get divorced?' I guess I asked her lots of times. She said that everybody would be happier that way. She said that we would be unhappy children if they stayed together. Sometimes I cry."

How do children of divorce cope with visitation rights? How do they relate to their divorced parent's new spouse or girlfriend or boyfriend?

Larry said, "We visit Daddy about once a month or maybe not so much. Sometimes we call him. The only time he calls us is when he needs to talk to Mommy. Or Mommy needs to talk to him."

"And he never forgets my birthday or Christmas," added Gretchen.

How do they like the woman their daddy married?

"Well, she's not the nicest person in the world," commented Gretchen. "I mean I don't think she's as nice as

Daddy is. Sometimes I don't get along with her. Sometimes I'd like to be alone with Daddy."

Do they like living with their mom alone?

"We're not alone. We have two people living upstairs. Suzy and Cal. Suzy goes to school. There's two bedrooms. I like Cal. He comes down here a lot. I don't think of him as a father. Well, sometimes. I call Cal 'Cal' and when he helps me with homework and stuff like that, he's like a father."

"I just don't think that Cal is my father, because I already have one," added daddy's girl.

"Sometimes he tells us what to do, but he tells us the wrong thing and Mommy corrects him. Sometimes he spanks me."

Would they want Mom to marry Cal?

"I wouldn't. He's not my father," repeated Gretchen. "He's just a friend still. I like it with Mommy. I just wouldn't want there to be a stepfather for me."

"I'd like to have a father living with me." One evening at dinner Larry asked his mother to marry Cal so that he could tell his friends that he had a father. Once he commented to a friend at the door, "I have two fathers." He wanted it to be true. He was embarrassed and didn't know how to explain Cal's presence.

"None of My Friends Ever Got a Divorce or Anything"

Children ages 8 to 11 see everything and hear every word in the drama of their parents' divorce. They may even become engrossed in the action. But some of the meanings are still lost on them and they experience the feelings of hurt and pain and confusion.

Three years ago when Lisa was 12 and June 10 their parents divorced. They shared their feelings freely.

"We were sitting on the couch and they both told me.

I ran crying into my room," remembered Lisa.

"I just sat there," June said. "I didn't know what to do."

"None of my friends where I used to live ever got a divorce or anything," Lisa commented.

"We lived in a very old established area," June explained. "Grandma didn't help either. She lived only a block away. We were the first family divorce. Grandma said that Mom disgraced the whole family."

"Well, it's a whole new idea. You don't think it's going to happen to you, and when it does it's a shock. I was in a world of my own," continued Lisa. "I cried. I was off by myself. When we moved out here I made new friends, and they understood because they had been through the same thing."

The girls visited their father every other weekend. When they returned home they were sick for a week.

"I was just emotional."

"Nerves. I wouldn't talk. It's like coming back from one parent's house into your house, and you get a very strange feeling."

"I felt like a Ping-Pong ball, from the one to the other," added Lisa.

"You'd come back and wonder should you tell your mom about something. You don't know what to say."

"Like my mom is married to Luke now and my dad is dating other people. But I feel kind of uneasy seeing them together here in this house when he comes to get us. And I think Mom feels uneasy having him here."

"Usually he doesn't come in when he drops us off," said June. "He just drops us off and leaves. I don't like to remember these things." She was practically in tears. "I get kind of sad."

Lisa came to the rescue.

"I guess my folks divorced because Mom was really

17

nervous and everything. She was going to a counselor, and he said that she should get rid of her problems. I don't know if that's true. That's what Grandma told me. I'm afraid to ask."

"It really hurt me 'cause I was really close to my dad." June was in tears again.

"I was never really close to my dad until the divorce, but now I'm really close to him. I kind of resented my mom," added Lisa.

"I did too. I think she broke up the home. That's what I feel. I have to live with Mom and it was really hard. I did want to go with my dad, but he couldn't take care of us anyway."

"I love my dad. It was hard on him what Mom did."

During these growing years children grasp more of what happens to the grown-ups around them. Their emotions are keen. They may take sides. They may swing from one to the other in their allegiance. They feel caught in some very tense situations. Confusion, frustration, hurt, pain, hostility, resentment, rejection, fear, and discouragement may become part of their emotional agenda. Their inability to understand the total reality —although they're trying hard to understand—leaves them in a no-man's-land still desiring both parents. (This depends on the type of family life they have known.)

The unsettling experiences of divorce may submerge only to surface later in the rebellious teens, when natural rebellion mixed with buried pain and confusion are released upon the struggling parent who retains custody; a custody for which the youngster may be both grateful and resentful. Resentful because there is only one parent left in his everyday life.

Katie was 9 and her sister Cheryl was 13 when their parents divorced. Their father simply announced to their mother that he was leaving; there was another woman. Within a month after the divorce their father remarried.

"I didn't understand what he was telling us," said the younger Katie.

"I just didn't believe it," answered Cheryl. "It's still like a dream. I know it's happened. There's nothing I can do about it. Just a week before, I told my friends that I never thought my parents would get a divorce. Later I was furious. I cried a lot. I was really mad at him for doing it."

"I really didn't know what he was saying," volunteered Katie. "Dad ran upstairs. He was crying. I asked him, 'What's the matter?' He said, 'I'll tell you later.' "

Katie sees her father about once a month, but Cheryl refuses. "I don't want to see him. It's really not him personally, it's what he *did*. I feel sorry for Mom. I'm in a bad mood even when my dad calls on the phone. I don't want to talk to him. Most of the time I just hang up on him."

"Mom never said anything bad about him, or that we shouldn't go see him," said Katie.

"Why should I feel an obligation to see him, when he didn't feel the responsibility or whatever to stay with us?" asked Cheryl. "I know he wants to see both Katie and me, but he has his own family now.

"Dad always wants us to go with him and his wife. He always says that we're a family and she's your mother. Or he says 'stepmother.' But she isn't my mother and she isn't my stepmother either. She's just a lady who married my dad!

"I have a close friend in junior high. She's my teacher. She takes us out for lunch and I can really talk to her. I've grown spiritually. It's helped my loneliness. I'm closer to God," said Cheryl.

"Once I was in my reading group and I started crying," added Katie. "But I don't cry anymore at school."

Do they want their mother to remarry?

"I do and I don't. I don't want it to happen again," Katie was the first to answer.

"If Mom remarries that's her business," responded Cheryl. "I'm not going to say, 'No you can't.' It's up to her. I don't want her to feel an obligation to us, that she can't get married again because of us. But I don't want her to marry some weirdo. My dad sure married a weird person."

In time Cheryl will visit with her father again, but for now the hurt is still too fresh.

"Mom and Dad Had a Perfect Marriage, But..."

Teenagers' reactions to divorce are probably as varied as the teens are. No one pattern emerges. Some act subdued, some become downright resentful, difficult, rebellious, others go so far as to refuse to see, visit, call or even contact the departed parent. (That may last for about a year, although some may remain obstinate longer.) The rebellion may extend to their schoolwork which soon dips to zero. They can take up with the wrong crowd and become involved in the worst things. Some will demand their independence, voice their frustrations and blatantly act out their hostilities.

On the other hand there are teens who rally to the side of the parent with whom they live, help around the house, pick up the pieces, and become a stabilizing strength to a mother who has to go out and work for a living. Sometimes they grow stronger in their faith while leaning heavily on their friends at church.

The teen years are an unsettling time. If their family life has been relatively secure, providing warmth and faith, the young people's questions dig even deeper.

20

One teenager who summarized many concerns that children of divorce have is April, a vivacious 18-year-old whose parents had been divorced three years. April accepted the events in her life with unusual faith:

"It seems like a long time ago! I just had lunch with my dad yesterday. Either he calls me or I call him and we'll have lunch about once a month." Her father is remarried to a woman with two daughters. "I like her two daughters. They're 17 and 16. I never had any sisters. I think of them as sisters, kind of. But I don't do things with them. Dad is the one I really care about.

"You know, Mom and Dad had a perfect marriage. They never fought at all. Dad always went to his room when he was upset and Mom went to be alone. The day when I came walking downstairs and Mom said, 'Dad left last night,' I just went, 'Huh?' I was in shock. I never thought anything like that would happen. The next day my dad picked me up and talked to me. He said, 'I don't love your mother anymore.' "

Today, rethinking the events still upsets April. "What could I say? He was almost like a stranger to me, saying those strange words. I looked at him and thought, 'You're Dad? You're the same person who was at our house 24 hours ago watching TV with me?' He seemed like somebody else. He did tell me he was going to get a divorce, which Mom didn't know at the time. So I started preparing myself. Then I found out about the other woman. He told Mom about a month later."

How did April feel about that?

"I was almost glad that there was some kind of an excuse! I'm not saying that Jane was an excuse. But I'm saying you grow out of love. How do you grow out of love? I can't understand that. After 19 years? Maybe if he had hit her once in a while, or she walked out on Dad. But things were so beautiful."

21

She took a deep breath. "Dad's a lot happier now. I don't think he was ready for two extra kids. But that's what came with her. I *think* he's happier. Every time we have lunch I try to look at him and see behind his eyes. He covers it all up with talk about business. He's very proud of me. I'll always be his little girl. I graduated from high school with good grades. One of his daughters is in continuation school and the other one is practically flunking. I'm the one with the good grades. My dad will do anything for me. And I love him more now than when he was living with us."

She smiled, "Took me a while! I just didn't wake up and say, 'I love him more now!' I had to struggle with myself. I had a lot of people around that helped me— one older guy at church, he was 22. At 16 that's very old. I went to a Bible study. He was the leader and we got very close. I talked a lot to him. I was having a hard time accepting how much Dad hurt Mom. She had to go through the hospital—psychiatrists—and I had to live with two aunts. I blamed it all on Dad. I saw her tears, her sleepless nights, and wanting to kill herself. I remember Mom wanting to buy a gun and asking, 'Can you make it on your own?' She asked me that! 'No, I can't make it on my own. I need you. Don't leave me.' "

April sighed deeply. "I really could have gone off the deep end. Sixteen is a kind of age when everything affects you so much. But I got stronger in my faith. The guy who helped me a lot had a Christian background. I became a Christian when I was seven. I never lost my faith. It just got much stronger. I still go to the same church and see those same people."

Her mother has met some men.

"I like Chuck. He is the only guy I've liked that she's gone out with. The first two I had a hard time accepting. Last night when I came home Mom and I sat down and

22

talked about Chuck and my boyfriend, Randy. It's unusual to talk about dating problems with your mother —who she goes out with, who I go out with, when she comes home, when I come home. We kind of tease each other about that. You know, when Dad left I was really down on guys. I didn't trust any of them. I would go out with one and think, 'You're not going to leave me like my father.' But I'm over that now."

Is she planning to marry?

April laughed. "Oh, sure, I plan to get married. I'll marry a Christian for sure. If I marry a Christian man I hope we work out our problems. There'll be no divorce. I don't even think about divorcing. Mom has given me a lot of freedom. Mom trusts me. I won't go to bed with a guy and she knows that. I'm saving myself for that one man I'm going to marry."

Will You Be Able to Help Them Cope?

The basic question in this chapter is, *What does divorce do to the kids?* The answer is, *Plenty!* Sometimes it's devastating. Some children, when suddenly and severly jostled out of their secure family situations, do not possess the tools with which to cope. They grope, they struggle, they ponder. Sometimes they go off the deep end and wind up in antisocial, antiauthoritarian behavior.

Before the divorce there had been tension and difficulty in Jimmy's home. His parents were driven apart by day-to-day differences in the rearing of their children. Jimmy's mother witnessed the personality change of her once easy-to-love, obedient son, soon after the divorce. Jimmy had been obedient because he feared his father's outbursts. However, a cool defiance had been smoldering beneath his masked obedience. Jimmy refused to accept his mother's authority. He dropped his church buddies and became a leader in a group of kids involved in drugs and alcohol. Later he was thrown out of two junior high schools in the eighth grade.

Was Jimmy's far-out erratic behavior a cover-up for the broken dreams of his shattered world? Did he understand why he hurt so much? No! He covered it with defiance until he began to mature and accept some responsibility for his life. The turn for the better did not occur until three years later. Then improvement came very slowly. Although he still argues that there is no God, he is beginning to show by his actions the influence of Christian teachings he received as a younger child.

Yet who is to say what the facing of family problems will do for young people in the long run? Could these trials mold them into better persons, more aware of life's problems, more capable of coping in crisis, more trusting in God? Perhaps those children who have come to terms with tough realities are the better for it in later life. Perhaps they have gained valuable experiences the hard way. But they have gained them nevertheless.

April—whose parents had a "perfect" marriage until it fell apart—found help in God, in her church, in her friends and within herself. She asked her parents probing questions to help herself understand their divorce. All children and teenagers want answers. Some are afraid to ask. Fortunate is the child or teenager who can communicate their fears and questions to their parent and receive wise help and answers.

But how will you be able to give those wise answers? Will you be able to help them cope, because *you* are able to cope? The first step is to take the controls of your life.

2

You Can Take Control of Your Life

Divorce is a trying experience for everyone concerned. What can the divorced parent do? How are you going to handle the children? How do you deal with those in the broken family who are having an especially rough time? How do you handle *yourself*?

The key is in your emotional health. It's up to you to get it all together by putting yourself at the controls of your life. Only *you* can do this. The sooner you get hold of yourself the better. You are in charge of your destiny. When you live out your faith with certainty and underlying security, your children will feel peace and love. They will respond when you assure them, by all you are and do, that you're in charge. They need consistent strength from you.

Were you in charge of your emotional makeup before? If you were, then you can be in charge of your emotions again. If you were not, you may need help. Seek it. If you were a peaceful, self-assured person, then you're able to be that person again. You are no different. You are still *you*. You will be in charge because you have been in charge before. You have been temporarily derailed by these events but you can get back on the track of self-assurance. When you do, you will discover that you're a better, more mature person, more confident and loving than you were before. That's worth striving for!

To gain control of yourself you need to recognize and define your feelings and emotions. There are normal stages a person travels through during the time of trauma. One of them is the experience of shock, dismay, panic—which can lead into depression and self-pity. The trauma of divorce is a tearing-apart. These feelings are normal, because you are human. And God understands. He made you with emotions. Don't deny your emotional makeup. However there is potential danger ahead. The sooner you emerge from each stage the better it will be for you and your children. When you capitulate to these devastating feelings you will not be in charge. These feelings can take over; and if they're allowed to rule you, they can turn your life into ruin.

"I'm trying to keep my head together while I struggle with my divorce." Paula, a 28-year-old mother of two children, shared. "I cry out, 'Why me?' My heart is breaking. I want to be the mother my children deserve. I want to discover the person I was before I was labeled wife and mother, as if that label eliminated me as a person in my own right. Sometime soon the sun will shine on me again. Love is in my future, of that I feel certain. I *can* find myself."

Paula and others who have suffered the problems of

divorce can find very practical help in the writings of Paul, the apostle, to the Philippians. Paul was not writing these words specifically to divorced families, but their application is obvious. There are steps you can take right now to regain control of your life or to strengthen progress you have already made.

> *Delight yourselves in the Lord, yes, find your joy in him at all times. Have a reputation for being reasonable, and never forget the nearness of your Lord. Don't worry over anything whatever; whenever you pray tell God every detail of your needs in thankful prayer, and the peace of God, which surpasses human understanding, will keep constant guard over your hearts and minds as they rest in Christ Jesus. . . . If you value the approval of God, fix your minds on whatever is true and honourable and just and pure and lovely and admirable. Put into practice what you have learned from me and what I passed on to you, both what you heard from me and what you saw in me, and the peace of God will be with you. . . . I have learned to be content, whatever the circumstances may be. I know now how to live when things are difficult and I know how to live when things are prosperous. In general and in particular I have learned the secret of eating well or going hungry—of facing either plenty or poverty. I am ready for anything through the strength of the One who lives within me* (Phil. 4:4-13, *Phillips*).

Paul tells us several things in this passage that can help you regain control. These are:

No more self-pity—"Delight yourselves in *the Lord*, yes, find your joy in him at all times" (v. 4);

27

Don't worry—"Don't worry over anything whatever" (v. 6);

Think positive thoughts—"Fix your minds on whatever is true and honourable and just and pure and lovely and admirable" (v. 8);

Be Content—"I have learned to be content, whatever the circumstances may be" (v. 11);

Set goals—"I can do all things in him who strengthens me" (v. 13, *RSV*).

No More Self-Pity

The waters of self-pity can mingle with the waters of depression to form a slimy pool. The waters of guilt also flow into the pool, and when enough of those waters join together they overflow into a river of grief. First we feel sorry for ourselves. Then we grieve for ourselves, accentuate our failures, feed our rejection, mull over the loss of the marriage, overrate the poor example we've been as Christians and greatly magnify our miserable condition.

A self-pitying person becomes rather small—just for "me, myself and I." But we aren't alone. Our children are traveling in the same canoe with us down those muddy rivers. They are aware of our wallowing and purposelessness, and they hardly know what to do. They may say a word here or there (sometimes full of wisdom) but we are flowing along at such a clip that we don't take it to heart. We hardly even hear them as we dive again into our pool of self-pity, practically drowning in our misery.

The longer we thrash about in these troubled waters, the longer we splash our children with our insecurities and troubles. None of us is becoming whole.

How can you forsake self-pity? Paul says to "delight yourselves in the Lord, yes, find your joy in him at all times. Have a reputation for being reasonable, and never forget the nearness of your Lord" (Phil. 4:4,5).

On the surface this sounds ridiculous. How can you find joy when nothing in your life is conducive to rejoicing or to joy? Paul often had nothing to rejoice about but he said, "I know now how to live when things are difficult and I know how to live when things are prosperous . . . I am ready for anything through the strength of the One who lives within me" (Phil. 4:12,13). The key to this kind of rejoicing is in the phrase "in the Lord." When you are secure about your position in Christ, when you can identify that you are part of His eternal purposes and are related to Him, then you can begin to *rejoice*.

Don't Worry

As a divorced person you suddenly find that you are alone in worries that you were once able to share with your mate. The usual problems of money, security, business matters, and so forth, are minor compared to the worry over your children. When Paul told us to not "worry over anything whatever," he meant the problems associated with our children as well.

How can you stop worrying when your child is in trouble? Dean tells about his period of adjustment after his parents divorced: "I didn't think ahead of the consequences when they divorced. I just accepted it. When I first went with my mom she had a hard time handling me. With father I got away with more. As a kid I think I was very egotistical, I wasn't afraid of anything. I had long hair, I said anything I wanted, I did anything I wanted to. Hardly any parental control. I wasn't worried about getting enough love. I didn't even think of that. I just went on my own. I got into lots of trouble at school. I just loved that! I had a ball and went crazy. I

29

got arrested for possession of marijuana four times, when I was 16, or 17. Kids in married families get in trouble smoking pot too, but I didn't start until after the divorce."

Kids do act up. Just when they could help keep life smooth at home, they themselves hurt too much to be of help. A divorce may severely accentuate their insecurity. For many teenagers the growing-up problems are already present—no longer a child, not yet an adult —which means not all their problems are related to the divorce! It is both foolish and unnecessary to blame yourself when a placid preteener turns to be a hellion come junior high school.

Don't worry! Spiritual and emotional health is a prerequisite for helping our children. Too often we wind up like the mother who confessed: "They're driving me crazy. Skip is constantly sick and out of school. I have to go to work and I don't like leaving an 11-year-old at home by himself. But what can I do? When Gordie comes home the two of them fight all the time. I was called in to see the school counselor for the first time, because Gordie is causing trouble on the playground."

These periods will not last forever. They are phases. They may seem to linger, but when children sense steadfastness, patience, understanding and love on your part, they will get on the right path again. To be sure, for some it takes much longer than for others. Don't be too hard on yourself if your children do not react according to *your predetermined expectations.* It may, in fact, help if you change your expectations.

Allow kids to express their feelings. Give them this freedom without retaliation, recrimination or punishment. It's risky but healthy. As one 13-year-old girl said to her mother: "What do you know about teenagers? You've never had one before." That may sound disrespectful to you, but allow them such free expression. It will help them overcome their hostilities.

"I'm always aggressive," confessed Drew. "I was the discipline problem. Now that I look back I realize I don't often think in terms of other people. I don't consider how other people think or feel. I was a very unruly 14-year-old. I got into trouble. I picked fights. My dad was constantly after me. I was such an unruly kid that I wouldn't let him punish me. I wouldn't talk to my dad for a couple of weeks."

When parents themselves endure the sufferings of divorce, experience their own anger, feel their own pain and are too upset to face their own heartaches, their children's problems intensify! These problems then compound the parents' frustrations. A vicious circle is set in motion. Parents, worried over their children, confused at their behavior and anxious about what will happen, only add to their children's burdens.

How do you cope when your son or daughter has problems such as these? The answer doesn't lie in worry; the answer lies in what Paul tells us next: "Tell God every detail of your needs in thankful prayer, and the peace of God, which surpasses human understanding, will keep constant guard over your hearts and minds as they rest in Christ Jesus" (Phil. 4:6,7).

Does the Word of God work only when everything is placid? Can we be in peace only when all the circumstances are under control? Jesus found peace in the midst of the storm on the sea of Galilee while the disciples became frantic. How did He manage that? He had a deep faith in God, His Father, and He lived by that faith at the center of His life.

Worry is a lack of trust. Worry stirs us up within when, instead, we could be relying on God. The circumstances may be most imperfect around us. A child of

31

divorce may be getting into trouble, as Dean did, or rocking the home in other ways. We will have to deal with those circumstances. We will have to find ways to calm the storm.

But the truth is that even in the storm we can be free from worry. Since the calming effect comes from God and the peace He creates comes from within ourselves, it is possible to be in charge of our lives and thereby help our children the most!

You hope that your son or daughter who has been damaged by the divorce will yet grow up to become a fine human being. Keep that goal in view. That's what you're aiming for. In time they will emerge from their erratic behavior patterns because they have to find themselves too. Give them room to grow, and time, with plenty of compassionate understanding tossed in.

Above all, don't worry. "Tell God every detail of your needs in thankful prayer, and the peace of God, which surpasses human understanding, will keep constant guard over your hearts and minds as they rest in Christ Jesus" (Phil. 4:6, *Phillips*).

Think Positive Thoughts

"If you believe in goodness and if you value the approval of God, fix your minds on whatever is true and honourable and just and pure and lovely and admirable. Put into practice what you have learned from me and what I passed on to you, both what you have heard from me and what you saw in me, and the God of peace will be with you" (Phil. 4:8,9).

After wallowing in the muddy waters of divorce, many of us find it difficult to think thoughts that are anything like these Paul describes. We tend to dwell on our hurts and disappointments, remembering words that were spoken in anger and actions that were intended to destroy us. We become angry, resentful, hostile and ready to explode. Unless we change our direction, reprogram our thoughts, this attitude can lead to destruction for ourselves and for our children.

Anger can become so fierce that it can blow up in your face. You may be prompted to do mean and destructive things. A meek and quiet wife may be utterly surprised to find herself exploding in the lawyer's office, demanding "to take him for all he's worth." A mild-mannered man may experience the desire to crash his car when a defiant mood overtakes him. He wants to rid himself of all his pressing hostility. Unfortunately some destroy themselves!

Often anger is a way out of depression. It can be a positive force. But you must channel the anger into constructive action. Accept the anger, the hurts and the truth and keep on moving. Don't stop. You are passing through dangerous territory. Eventually you must assume control of your emotions, rechannel your thoughts and seek the beautiful, lush, green valley that David spoke of in Psalm 23. The sooner you arrive in the valley, the better it will be. The peaceful and prosperous valley is the place where you accept yourself, your divorce and your particular circumstances. This is what God wants for you and He will help you stay there if you will trust Him. You are God's child. He loves you.

If you doubt that love, look again at the ministry of Jesus. Jesus is the Son of God. He exemplifies God's love and care in His life and ministry. Jesus didn't turn anyone away. All those who came to Him were received. Even if you feel like a prodigal son (although there is no reason why you need to feel like that because of a divorce), the prodigal can always return home. You will be received with open arms by a loving Father. That's the way it is. That's the way Jesus tells it. And that's what He demonstrates by all His actions. You can accept yourself because He accepts you. He accepts you in love. He accepts you freely, completely and without any strings. He died for you!

When you accept yourself because He accepts you, you will radiate self-confidence. You will think the positive thoughts Paul spoke of. Your children will respond to the confident you. Then you "will find that the God of peace will be with you."

Be Content

"For I have learned to be content, whatever the circumstances may be. I know now how to live when things are difficult and I know how to live when things are prosperous" (Phil. 4:11,12).

This statement of Paul's is even more extraordinary when we realize that he wrote these words while he was a prisoner. He was certainly going through some "difficult" times, yet he remained content. This advice is especially important to the divorced person because many of them find themselves in difficult financial circumstances. There isn't as much money as there was before, and the children may suffer.

Angela, of whom we spoke in chapter 1, was able to accept this problem: "If we don't see Daddy for a long time we phone him. Mom talks to him too. They're still friends. Like, well, usually when you get divorced, the mother ends up with the child, and the father has to send some money. We talked to him about a little more money, but he said he didn't have it. So we get by. I *would* like some more things at Christmas, but what I get is what I get!"

"There just wasn't any money. I branded myself from that time on as *poor*," recalled 17-year-old Tish. "Dad supported us for a while. Then he stopped. It irked my

34

mother to ask, so she finally said, 'Forget it.' Mom never took him to court. I, too, became self-reliant; I went to work soon after I was 15, and I've been working ever since."

Like Tish and her mother you are in charge. Whatever your decision, it is necessary to be inwardly content. The apostle Paul found contentment in riches and in poverty. The amount of money did not dictate his contentment. How did he manage that?

Contentment is a fruit of the Spirit. We sometimes call it *joy*. As God's Spirit dwells in you, you will be more and more filled with inner contentment. Trust Him even in the midst of your trying circumstances, allow His Spirit to guide you in your decisions, seek His help and act on His leading. Teach your children contentment, not materialism, by your example.

Set Goals

"I can do all things in him who strengthens me" (Phil. 4:13, *RSV*). When you have forsaken self-pity, learned to control worry and are on your way to thinking positive thoughts, then you are beginning to gain control of your life. "But," you say, "the Lord must be at the controls of my life." That's true. Jesus Christ is to be Lord. But the Lord does not deny us our responsibility. He will not do for us what we must do for ourselves! As Lord of our lives He gives us the responsibility to live, to act, to be and to worship. Now is the time to set some goals for your life. No one else will be allowed that place of power.

Ask yourself some questions: Do I need to get more education? Do I need to find a job? A better job? Do I need to lose weight? Do I want to start a program of exercising? Do I need to make new friends? Do I need to establish regular Bible reading? Prayer time? Church attendance? What goals do I need to establish for myself?

Once you establish your needs, you can begin to write down your goals. Determine how you can attain your goals. When you have determined and planned how you will *attain* your goals, post them where you will see them daily. Keep in your mind the vision of the person you want to become. Be good to yourself by working on your goals. As your needs change, adjust your goals. As you attain each goal, draw a line through it and chart your progress. Progress comes with work and direction, and your self-esteem will soar.

I can do all things through Christ. Paul puts himself in charge of his life. He affirms he can do everything. Not just a few things but all things. Yes, the power comes through the presence of Jesus Christ, the one who lives within him, but Paul himself can do it! He is very confident. The wheel of his life is in his own hands. He will not surrender to any destructive forces even while he remains locked up in prison.

The sooner you assume control of yourself, your outlook and your feelings, the sooner you can take charge of your home and help your children. Then you will experience peace, the peace God wants for you.

Peace Can Be Yours

The more at peace you are within, the more your family will respond to your peace. Yes, it will take time. You cannot hurry it along. But consider this: Of the various stages described in this brief chapter, which is the best? Where do you want to be? In the muddy pool? Navigating the stormy river? Traversing the rough roads? Or enjoying the peaceful valley? If, therefore, you're in control of your feelings and you desire peace, who will keep you from your goal? It's up to you. Take the reins of your life. No one else will bring you to the promised land, but *you can* reach it. Yes, you can!

Peace is not just a gift. It is the outgrowth of the life of God in you. One of the fruit of the Spirit is peace. This is a time for you to claim that fruit and to enter the valley that lies beyond your struggles. Then you will know that, with God's help, you are at the controls of your life.

Part II

Building a Single-Parent Family

3
Where Do We Begin?

As you probably already know, building a single-parent family is not always easy. Many find it extremely difficult and trying. Children and young people often become emotionally damaged because of their parents' problems. It seems as if their whole world has crumbled! The security they have always known and taken for granted is no more.

So if you're newly divorced, or if you have already lost several rounds in the battle to build a one-parent home, what are some of the answers? As a matter of fact, what really are some of the problems?

Understand that Children Don't Like Changes

One of the biggest problems is that children don't take to changes very readily, especially changes that affect their sense of security.

Melissa and Terry lived with their mother through a lengthy, drawn-out court battle that lasted two years. Their mother informed us that for the first three months Terry, who was seven, refused to see his father. Terry himself told us, "I was very happy when my dad left. He's not here to tell me what to do! I don't enjoy seeing my father on Saturdays."

Melissa said, "I didn't like the big, new house Daddy bought, but I like the swimming pool. Sometimes my dad would bring our bags to the school office. And I hated that. I felt embarrassed carrying this bag after school. He didn't want to drive to the apartment. I would stand with my bag in front of the school and wait for my mother."

Her mother told us that Melissa stuttered for about four months after the separation. Terry had been very belligerent and was often hard to manage. Both kids calmed down when Mom gained a firm grip on her own life!

For Peter who was nine and Esther who was six, the divorce was very fresh. Only a year had transpired and for at least six months both children had difficulties adjusting.

"I didn't understand why Dad had to leave," said Peter. "They told me that I wouldn't understand why. They just said it would be best if they didn't live together. I didn't feel too good at first. Sometimes I cried. Sometimes I just stayed in my room."

"Some of my friends knew that my parents were separated. I wish Mommy and Daddy were back together," Esther confided.

After they visit with their father their mother notices the changes. It takes them almost a day to settle down. Before their father arrives Peter is sometimes in tears.

"Sometimes I feel bad when I get back home. I feel

bad for Daddy. I feel sorry for him," said Esther.

"I feel bad 'cause I have to leave the house and go somewhere with Daddy. I wish he could just live here. Sometimes I get upset with the way Daddy drives. One time he was tired and we were driving home. I was sitting in the front seat. He started to go off the wrong exit. And he was going over 65. Then we went down the wrong street."

Peter has been going to a child-guidance clinic. "Sometimes we talk and sometimes we play games. I worry about Mommy. I guess at first I felt I was to blame for the divorce. I told them that. But I don't have anything to do with it. I learned that."

But things are changing. Peter's report card this year is the best he's ever brought home.

Get Involved with Your Children's Pain

While children are struggling with changes in their own lives, parents are often too preoccupied with the business of adjustment to notice. Sometimes they are suffering with such a deep self-pity they don't want to see their children's inner pain.

When the children kick up a little fuss, the parent tries to quiet them down. The troubled parent fails to see that, behind the silence, the retreat, the rebellion and the sometimes verbal abuse, children may be confused, grieving, feeling guilty, insecure and unsure of themselves. If the children mask their true feelings, these feelings may emerge at a later time.

On the other hand if children express their frustrations, parents tend to think that their children are being unreasonable! "Why are the kids being so unreasonable? Don't they know what I'm going through? Don't they understand I'm suffering through the death of a marriage?"

Yes, your children do know something about that, but their ability to cope depends a great deal on how you handle yourself. As long as you're in tears they will be upset too. They get their signals from you. Aren't you the one to guide and encourage them? You're the adult. You have the experience.

Does it seem almost cruel to tell parents that they must lose their lives in order to find them? It is hard, when deep waters swirl around you, to have to lose your life for others. When you are in shock and despair you want to save your own life. But it *does* help to forget your own pain and become concerned enough to get involved in your children's pain.

Small children will not make many demands on you. They are quite ready to respond to encouragement. Preteens require more energy. Teenagers are another story. Some will respond when they know you care. If they sense your concern, they will feel free to express the inner turmoil they're experiencing.

Other teenagers may become rebellious. After having endured the stormy years of their parents' marriage, they will be "ticked off" by this latest happening. They often refuse to respond to kindness or concern. In fact, in their condition, nothing will reach them until they've worked through their hostilities by themselves.

Because they hurt they sometimes reject kindness, love, understanding and even a listening parent. Consider the reasons why they behave in such a rebellious manner.

Children and teenagers need to work off their hostilities. Does your teenager internalize? Does he become quiet? Retreat into his room? Run all the time with friends, trying to escape by going out almost every night? Can't he stand to be alone? Must he have the music constantly playing from the moment he gets up to the time he falls asleep? Does he lose his grip on his schoolwork? Does he become a discipline problem? Does he turn nasty? Use bad language? Is he openly defiant? Does he reject the standards you have set?

It isn't easy to accept these actions from your children, to persist patiently, to accept their rejections, to continue doing what you believe is right and honest and loving. But your children must release their pain somehow, somewhere, and you become the most likely target. By becoming that target, accepting those inflicted blows, absorbing their pain so they may be free of their burdens, you do, in part, lose yourself to find yourself.

The basic question you must ask is, *what is happening on the inside?* How can you, as a parent, approach the heart of the matter? Are you able to accept their pain and absorb their insecurity? How can you alleviate some of their hurt. Or do they just have to work their way through this without you?

Caring and loving and feeling along with a child or a teenager will not be rejected in the long run. Your loving touch is generally appreciated. So it is vital that you come up from the slough of despond so that you can encourage your children.

Follow Some Positive Steps

We have discovered at least six positive things you can do to help your children adjust to your divorce.

First, allow the children time to heal. It isn't going to happen overnight. You can't hurry a healing. As you need time, so do they. Allow them this adjustment period.

One parent has already left the family for whatever reasons. You are still there. Let your children know that you won't leave them, you believe in them, you trust them and you care. Form and maintain solid relationships with your children. Keep a good attitude and exert a great amount of patience.

The New Testament has quite a few things to say about patience—it's a fruit of the Spirit mentioned in Galatians 5:22. The writer of Hebrews tells us that we "have need of endurance [patience], so that you may do the will of God and receive what is promised" (10:36, *RSV*). The Old Testament often enjoins us to "wait on the Lord." Healing is not instantaneous. The deeper the wound, the longer it takes to heal, and this disruption in the home is not a little scratch but a very deep wound.

Don't reveal all your emotions. You need to share your feelings with someone, but don't dump the entire spectrum of your emotions on your children. Choose someone else. Your children cannot handle all of your emotions as well as their own. Even though your children are the nearest persons to you—perhaps the only ones you can talk to most of the time—they cannot carry your cumbersome load while they're trying to dispose of a lot of trauma of their own!

One disturbed daughter living alone with her mother revealed her mother's bizarre, frightening emotions. She confided: "I'm glad my mom doesn't act crazy anymore. She almost drove the car with me in it over the side of the road into the canyon. And, do you know, she doesn't even remember the danger we were in?"

One mother said to us: "Sometimes it is easier to be unhappy than to deal with my emotions." That sounds self-defeating, but it's honest. To be in charge of yourself does not imply becoming a stoic who is so rigid that he hides his humanity. You don't have to mask your feelings and lock them in a safe. Not at all.

When you hurt so badly, you want others to know how much you've been wronged and how and why you hurt! If you must let it out (and you definitely need to

44

release pent-up emotions), talk to a friend or get some counseling. You need help in crisis, but spare your children.

Treat your children as persons. Children are growing up much faster these days. They're not yet adults in their early teens but they are persons. They need someone to understand, guide and sympathize with them in the struggles they're experiencing. They don't need someone to jump on, yell at or punish them for every act of misbehavior.

"My 12-year-old likes to wear dirty old clothes and he screams at me when I insist he change his outfit." So he screams at you, and you probably scream back. Isn't it important to avoid those verbal duels? Go into his room after he is asleep, take out those dirty clothes, throw them in the washer and make sure he has clean clothes to wear the next day. He'll wear them. You don't need those yelling matches and you won't have to nag him about clean clothes anymore!

Manny, 13 years old, was giving his advice to other children as well as talking about himself: "I would tell kids to love their parents. To be affectionate. Because their parents must be going through a lot of emotions. Divorce is a lot of strain on kids because they're asked to do things they normally don't have to do. And their parents have all this pent-up stuff inside. So they take it out on the kids. And the kids wonder, 'Why are they yelling at me?' I don't know why they do that! Why do they want to take their hatred out on children?"

Children want to be treated as persons!

Be honest. Explain things. "The children had no idea we were separating, because we never did argue," said Phyllis as she told us about her divorce. "There were no tears from Dotty who was nine. Dale who was six last year was angrier. I told them their daddy is an alcoholic.

I said that he started off with a problem and he can't stop. At this point I have forbidden the children to go to his home because I found out that he was drinking at home, and this upsets them. They were not getting any attention from him. There were also times when their father promised to come but didn't. The children would sit on the front step, waiting, running back in the house every 10 minutes to see if he had called. Then the phone would ring—their father just woke up. Two hours later another call—he hadn't left yet. Another hour—he wasn't coming! I tried to explain that it was Daddy's illness, but Dale would lie on the floor crying his eyes out. That was hard."

Children will accept the truth. If children do not hear the truth, if you don't explain why something happened, their minds will fantasize and often they blame themselves for the problems. If you begin to shade matters and they discover you lied, their trust in you will begin to fade. They need to believe in you, especially now when they're passing through doubts concerning one of their parents. Half of their security is out of the home. If they can't believe you, then who can they trust in this deceitful world?

This does not mean that you tell them every detail of every issue. You don't have to go round for round with them concerning what happened in the lawyer's office, court fights over custody, battles over property and all those payments. It is wise not to speak against the other parent. In extreme situations, when he or she is capable of malice, violence, driving and drinking, narcotics or criminal activity, then you need to protect your child with limited visitation rights or no visitation at all. Otherwise, encourage a positive relationship which is in the best interest of the child.

Don't destroy the other parent! It's easy to make the

other parent the bad guy because you have the children with you most of the time. You may want to retaliate because you were so severely hurt. But if you falsify, criticize unjustly or make too strong a case against your former mate, your child will soon find out the truth.

Don't put your ex-mate down. Consider the self-image of your children. Louise commented, "When my sister and her husband divorced they treated each other like dogs. My nieces and nephews were beginning to think they were puppies." Even though boys tend to be protective of their mothers, their self-esteem is linked to their fathers. Girls often feel sorry for Daddy because he lives alone in an apartment. But if her father makes derogatory statements about her mother, then the daughter's self-image is affected because she identifies with her mother. This is a time when your children need all the help you can give them in building a positive self-image.

Be discreet when you're talking on the phone. Be sure your children don't overhear what you don't want them to hear. Getting information secondhand this way can cause them to misunderstand and would jeopardize your relationship, and you don't need more trouble!

Speak the truth, don't feel you must tell every detail and don't slander your former mate.

A wise mother will handle situations as Nancy told us her mother did. "Mom always would tell us what was happening, but she didn't say anything bad about Dad. She didn't say that we shouldn't see him either. Even though he was involved with another woman before Mom and Dad were divorced." Nancy's mother has a great amount of integrity.

When Paul said to speak the truth in love (see Eph. 4:15) he was talking about all situations, even those personal relationships that are involved in divorce. Al-

47

ways speak the truth in love, no matter how much you feel you've been wronged!

Joni thought it best to keep as much as she could from her children. They were only four and two when the marriage broke up. She made sure the children didn't hear any arguments. When her husband moved out, she took the kids to relatives for the weekend. Joni never said a cross word about him no matter how much she hurt. Whenever the children asked why she was crying her stock answer was: "These are just happy tears!"

Kenny is 13 now, Sonya 11. "I don't remember when my father left. I don't remember anything. Mom told us that he had gone on a trip, and he'd come back soon. But he never did. I don't remember being really sad, though," said Kenny.

"Until we were older," added Sonya, "sometimes I'd cry and stuff. I missed Daddy, but any time we felt like talking to him, we just called him. I talk to him about once a week."

Their father has remarried. His wife is black.

"She usually doesn't go where we're going. She has her own things to do. I love her, in a way," answered Sonya. "Not as my own mother but as a good friend."

"We had known about Cecily. She was just a good friend. Mom didn't say anything about her. Then it just kind of dawned on us that he had married her."

"I didn't think much about her being black," continued Kenny. "As a matter-of-fact the only time I think much about the divorce at all is when I miss my dad. My mom gets sad because he left. I see her crying or depressed. And that makes me sad, and mad!"

"Mom is usually only sad when she's alone," commented Sonya.

Joni's Christian faith and life have been the stabilizing force in her children's lives. If children can draw closer to God during these conflicts their faith will grow into a greater reality.

Don't run interference for your former mate. Often a teenager decides that he or she cannot bear to see their father or mother. Encourage the teenager to call him or her to set up a time for visitation. Remain positive about your former mate, but you can't force the relationship between your children and their father or mother. Don't allow yourself to be placed in the middle. Let them make their own arrangements. It is best not to carry messages back and forth between them. You don't need to run interference or exert control.

Give your teenager time to work out his own problems. Chances are that he or she will be friends with their other parent again.

Give Your Children Quality Time

Your children need your support. Because you now have double responsibilities, your time is limited. But give them *quality* time. Let them know they can lean on you. Life may offer profound changes for children, but they become stronger as they're called on to endure those changes. As a result they will be better suited for life's crises.

Being thrust into a single-parent family life-style is not easy. It will be a big help to develop a philosophy for your home. Here are some questions to encourage you to think through basic issues. They are designed to aid you in formulating guidelines for the single-parent family.

Guidelines for Building a Happy, Harmonious Single-Family Home

Basic Attitudes—What kind of an atmosphere do we want to create in our home?

1. What is our main emphasis as a family? How will we change or strengthen this?
2. What am I telling the world and my children about myself by my life-style? How will I change or strengthen this?
3. What kind of memories will we all have as a result of living together in a single-parent home?
4. How can we become better listeners to each other?
5. Do we allow each other freedom of speech and the right to express different opinions?
6. Is our home a place of love? Of respect? Of courtesy? Of good manners?

Standards and Rules—Does everybody know what is expected of him as a member of this family?
1. What time is bedtime on school nights? On weekends?
2. How much television time can we allow each day?
3. How much time do we need for homework each day? How much does mom or dad get involved in homework?
4. What books and magazines will we have in our home? What reading material will not be permitted?
5. What family standards will we adopt for movies?
6. How will we handle issues such as alcohol, cigarette smoking, marijuana, etc.?
7. How much freedom can the teenagers in our home handle? What freedoms will they have?
8. When an adult is not at home, are the children and teenagers allowed to invite their friends into the house? Girls? Boys?
9. Do we agree on standards for clothes, hair, language? What compromises will we make?
10. What are our nutritional standards? Will we make any changes?

11. Do we say grace before meals at home? In restaurants?

The Parent's Responsibilities—What do I need to do to help my children mature?
1. How can I help my children be prepared for adulthood by the time they are legally adults?
2. How can I teach self-reliance?
3. What are my guidelines for discipline?
4. How will I reinforce good behavior? Discipline bad behavior?
5. How can I help my children develop their individual interests?
6. How can I deal with boredom when a child complains that there is nothing to do?
7. How will my children get their spending money? By allowance? By earning it? By need?
8. How will household responsibilities be delegated—chores inside the house; in the yard; training, feeding and cleaning-up after pets; etc.?

Parental Guidelines—Am I prepared to lead my family along established guidelines?
1. Will we attend church as a family? How many meetings a week or how many church activities can we handle as a family? As individuals?
2. Will we have family devotions? Encourage personal devotions?
3. What will our weekends be like? How much time will we set aside for chores? Family activities? Individual activities?
4. How will we celebrate birthdays? Holidays? Have I considered my children's mother/father, grandparents, aunts, uncles and other relatives on special days of the year?

5. Am I able to handle my finances? Should I budget my money? Can I afford credit cards? Is it necessary to cut expenses?
6. Can I teach self-control by example? How can I strengthen my own self-control?
7. When will I discuss sex with my children? Am I prepared to answer their questions about sex?
8. Who can I turn to in times of crises that can help me?

4

Marilyn: There Are No Easy Answers

Marilyn is the mother of two children. She shared with us how one parent can live out a Christian philosophy of life.

Marilyn draws people to herself. She is a leader, a thinker, a kind, understanding woman with personal charm. Life has not been easy for her. Her approach to the single-parent family shows insight into the needs of her children and herself.

How should parents explain divorce to their children?

"I suggest that parents be honest with their kids. Ask your child how he might feel if he had a friend that he didn't want to play with anymore. Then explain that's a little of what it's like for grown-ups to separate. Be honest from the very start.

"The scariest part of my divorce was *what is going to happen to my children?* Will they end up weird because of all this shake-up in their lives? My children love their father but I spend more time with them. I take time physically to hold them. I communicate with them. I have to make them feel secure. For a long time my son, who was six, couldn't make it out the door. He'd ask, 'Will you be here when I get home?' He would repeat the question several times. My daughter was eight and strong. She made up her mind that if her parents are to be divorced, she'll go along with it. She's a survivor, like me. She loves her father, but if she's going to be ignored when she sees him, she won't go. And that part annoys me, because he's not helping her to understand what men are like. I can't do that. I can tell her what God planned for us as a family without a father, but one of my great frustrations is that without a father she will not know what men are like. And a weak or withdrawn father will give her a poor father-image. I'm determined to allow some of the men in my family—brothers, cousins and others—to play a larger role in our lives."

Your husband turned out to be a weak man. Why did you marry him in the first place?

"I was looking for someone who was not like my father. I did not want a man walking all over me as my father did my mother. I was not going to be abused. My mother was beautiful and everyone loved her, but she was a martyr. After my mother died my father fell apart and I took care of him. But I couldn't stand that and, as he went down rapidly, I left because he was leaning on me. Then I met my husband in his gorgeous marine uniform. He was sweet and loving. He was strong. But a year after we married the roles reversed. He became dependent. He left the security of the uniform and showed himself to be a coward. Then the real me came out. I had unconsciously chosen a man I could handle and never be subjected to. His drinking, I thought, was part of the Marine Corps. But he is weak. He went from a strong mother to a strong wife. It's a pattern. That hurts. I didn't want to spend the rest of my life like that."

Marilyn believes she sacrificed herself to the marriage. Her husband made an excellent salary, bought suede shoes and expensive suits, while she survived in secondhand clothes! It was a pattern she had observed in her own family. Her father was a swanky lawyer who wore cashmere coats and Homburg hats, but there was not enough money to provide for the family of five children.

"I was repeating the cycle, until I realized that I'm valuable. I'm worth something. I should have some things too and I should have a sense of pride. When we came out West my mother-in-law gave him $5000 for a down payment for a house, but he blew it and that killed me—losing that house. Every time we got ahead he set us back. It wasn't deliberate, it was just his weakness. And each time I had to pull us back together again. I got tired of being the strong one. On the night before I told him I wanted a divorce I prayed: 'Lord, let me sleep tonight, but if this is what you want for my life, let me be strong for the decision I must make.' The next morning I told him I would not live this way, and I would not subject my children to this kind of life."

What affected you most in your divorce?

"Divorce has been more of a strain for me than for the children because I have a lot of pride. The hardest part has been giving up my children. You see, I had been a full-time mother. I've always believed I should be at home when they leave for school and when they come back. One of the first jobs I took forced me to leave by 7:45, and they didn't leave for school till 8:30. I set them down in front of the TV all dressed and ready, and I told them there was nothing to be afraid of. Just to go to school at 8:30. But it ate my guts out. I hated to do that to a six- and eight-year-old. No one to watch them.

"I know people talk about quality rather than quantity, but I'm a firm believer in being home when my child walks in from school at 3:00. They don't like it because I can't be here. I don't like it but *I have to accept it.* That's been hard for me. I'm stubborn. I look at all those other full-time mothers and I hate them. I call them *the cozies,* the ones with the cozy marriages. I can't go to any of the things they go to. I can't relate to them in any way, shape or form. I couldn't care less about the pattern of their china. It just doesn't relate. Life is much more serious for me now. It's a full-time job.

"I don't enjoy playing at night with my kids. That's because I'm literally beat when I come home from work. They like to play games with me and sometimes I do; we may play Scrabble, but it's an effort. Sometimes I do schoolwork with them. Sometimes we just sit together. We snuggle on the couch. Everything has to be done with them at night, but then friends call me. Two phone calls can tie me up all night. I can't hang up on people if they have an emergency. My divorced friends from church need someone to talk to, and I'm glad the Lord is using me to help. *It gives me self-worth.* I feel like a person, but I'm torn because of my family. My children need me and I get edgy. One kid is in the tub and the other is waiting. I can't talk on the phone all night!

"I can't even give one child my full attention. If one comes to me, the other one hangs around and listens to our conversation. Each one wants me alone, and that's not easy in a small place. They take turns sleeping with me. They just want to be close. And they measure everything—to a teaspoon! They won't let the other get more

56

of Mommy, won't let the other get ahead. I have to be a breadwinner, I need an adult relationship of my own, and house and children are too much for me. I overload myself, and that's one of my faults. Since I can't do everything I don't cook anymore. Just hamburgers and hot dogs, canned spaghetti and soup and sandwiches. That's all the time I have."

Have you had any problems supporting your family?

"I've got a college degree, but that isn't doing me a bit of good. I'm 34 and my age is against me since I've not had to work since college. There's a lot of competition out there. I'm holding a job in a private college nearby, but it's only $400 a month. Since my ex-husband is out of a job we're on welfare. So we have the food stamps and the medical and the whole bit. It's a bummer! I don't like it. I've never been on welfare in my life! Sometimes I don't believe it! In the meantime I'm looking for a good job. I've been interviewing for personnel assistant. That would pay about $950 a month and that would be heaven. This year I've let go of my kids bit by bit, getting them used to baby-sitters, getting them used to not having me here all the time, but it's still very hard on me."

Does your church help you cope with your problems as a single-parent?

"The married people have ignored all the divorced people in the church and just cast us aside. As soon as the husband is out of the picture, out we go too, with an occasional 'How're you doing?' But never, 'Could I take your kids one day for you? Is there anything I can do to help you?' What people don't realize is that for the divorced parent it's a tremendous responsibility to have the children all the time! You want to do all you can for your children, but you want to live your own life too. The gap between the marrieds and the divorced is as wide as the Grand Canyon. They don't know what goes on with us. As Christians they should keep us in the Body of Christ. We're being lost. I'm not, because I refuse to be lost, but there are lots of my divorced friends who don't make the effort any longer to belong to the fellowship of the church."

How are you helping your children to become adjusted to not having a father at home?

Marilyn is convinced that telling the truth to children is the only sane approach. They have to make up their own minds about the parent who has moved out. In her case she has encouraged the children to love him in spite of his problems. He is a gentle person and a kind father. If they decide not to love him that will be their decision, but they're facing this choice already in their young years.

"I will never make their father out to be anything he's not. They can't understand why he doesn't stop drinking. You just put the glass down and stop, so they think. Maybe when they're older they'll see. You know, we'll have to face the questions of marijuana and drinking later in their lives. I dread that. I dread the fact that they've seen this way of life and some of this can be hereditary. My husband got it from his father, and who knows that it won't go to my son? It's one of my concerns."

Marilyn doesn't think her daughter is open enough. She asked her recently what she thought about her father. The girl didn't know what to say. Then Marilyn suggested:

" 'If I were nine years old I'd be very sad that my father wasn't home.' That's when she opened up. She began to talk when she felt that I understood her. I verbalized her feelings. That's when quiet children begin to share. My young son has forgotten, thank God, most of last year, but he tore my guts out when his father didn't show up for visitation after promising to come. There were many times like that. But my son forgives quickly. We talked about that too and turned to God. I said, 'Maybe God has a plan for Daddy and we don't know what it is. And we have to wait it out. We have to be good to Daddy.' My son tells his friends that Daddy has another wife, that he has two wives. I try to explain that isn't right. He says, 'Well, I sort of think you're still married,' and I let it go at that point. He'll understand it some time."

How do you know how to answer the children's probing questions?

"I find that when I turn it over to the Lord, He really does give me the words to speak. It was agony for me that night to tell my children Daddy was leaving, but they ended up consoling me. I didn't want a divorce but I had to get a divorce— for the children's sake too. I prayed that my children would come out intact. Children must have some idea of what it feels like. Don't just say, 'Mom and Dad don't love each other,' because we do care for each other. Tell them, 'We just can't live together. It's better for us to live apart and you can still love us both. We will always be your parents, just as when you move away from home we will still be your parents. Both of us will work hard to make you happy, but Daddy won't be here and you will have to adjust.'

"I tried to sit with my children during quiet times without making it a question-and-answer session. I've been reading, in *Parent Effectiveness Training* [see Suggested Reading section], about how to communicate and that has helped. I've learned how to ask questions, not to put a child on the spot but to say, 'Gee, you look very sad today,' and usually they will respond to that but not to direct questions. I've also shared with them that Daddy had a hard time living with me. I was bossy. I was angry. I don't want to make him the bad guy because they will grow up thinking that men are rotten and women are fine, and I don't want that. It's not true. I want them to know I have faults. I sometimes use bad language, and they'll correct me and I'll apologize. Sometimes I get angry and they forgive me, and I think that takes down a lot of walls. Openness is probably the most important part of communication with children."

What about your family's spiritual development?

Marilyn has kept up the family devotions now that her husband is no longer the head of the home.

"We also say grace and I read to them from the Bible. But it is hard because life is so disjointed. There's nothing regular about it. Life-styles change. There is less time for everything, and then the things of God somehow get pushed away first. My son is very much into God and who He is, but my daughter isn't. She's more of a diplomat and just goes along. They know where I'm coming from and where I'm going. The Lord is very important in my life. I believe all we have to do is ask Him to help us to get some kind of guidance.

"I went to a weekend seminar and that was the weekend my husband asked me for the divorce papers so that he could get married again. I went completely to pieces in church. The church was full of people and I'm sobbing my head off uncontrollably. I went through a healing. A friend took me in her arms and prayed over me, and we went to the altar. I poured out my soul, my anger and hatred and resentment. I realized how very deep it was, all the pain and hurt I'd held in for almost 10 years, and what disillusionment has done to me. For me, faith comes slowly. I don't get the gift of things-happening-fast. I look back on this year and sometimes I think it's been a total waste. And yet I see the way I have matured, what has happened with my children, a new man I've come to love, and the Lord has let me have it a little bit at at a time. That's all I can take."

How are you building your own self-esteem?

"I feel like I'm just growing up at 34. I have to get to know me. Who am I? What have I to do with me? That's been painful. This is one of the traumas of the divorce—to come face-to-face with yourself. I'm not spending half a day preparing dinner anymore, getting his shirts to the cleaners, driving him to the train or the airport, changing diapers, running to the doctor. I think that's all I did in my marriage. I did nothing for me. I was probably a bore. So things are changing fast for me. I feel very capable. I'm learning to be in charge. I've started to listen to myself. I'm trying to accept where I am, and I'm not uncomfortable.

"One Saturday I should have cleaned my house, but I said, 'To heck with it.' I went shopping with my daughter. My son was with his father and I needed time with her alone. A friend of mine told me to take his charge card and buy myself some clothes. I had been very proud up to that point, but I decided pride was not getting me anywhere! I needed certain things. I was getting depressed because I had only one interview dress. I hadn't bought any clothes for myself for years. I was getting so sick of it. Everything had been taken away from me—time, the moments to get to know my kids intimately, because motherhood is terribly diminished."

Do you advise other parents?

"It's very hard to give other people advice, because people are so different. Their situations differ. Their relationships with their children are different. Some don't know how to talk to their kids. They keep on making the same stupid mistakes and push their kids away from them. Some are afraid. For example, there are parents who don't touch their children, or they touch them very little. If they gain custody, I don't know how they manage. I know another woman who isn't letting go of her divorce. She lives in the past and I can't talk to her anymore because she doesn't hear me, and her children suffer."

Do you think you will ever marry again?

Marilyn has learned much about herself in a short time. She knows she is not yet ready for a second marriage. She refuses to marry for a house and financial security. She has attended some groups. She has counseled with her pastor. She has helped others by her frankness. But it's the problem of her children that raises some questions for Marilyn's second marriage.

"The second time around you don't have the innocence you had the first time. The first time you were both blind, you had no strikes against you. But now I've got a family, I've already had a husband and married life. I'm not altogether sure I need another husband. For me, much as I love men and much as I love the man-woman relationship, it has to be an everyday thing. I've gotten very comfortable not having to struggle with another human being as I did for 10 years with my husband, because I feel I put out 150 percent and got back 30 percent. I never had a traditional marriage. So I'm probably afraid to make a commitment only to turn around a few months later to find that I'm bored again.

I don't want another divorce—*ever*. I will not marry anybody just to have a meal ticket. I need emotional security. I also need to know *I can make it on my own.*

"This whole question of remarriage is very serious. One father said to me, 'I didn't want some jerk bringing up my children.' That's why he hung around so long in his marriage. A divorced mother asked me, 'Whom can I trust to become a reliable father to my kids?' These are the concerns we all have. I couldn't handle dating lots of people. I didn't like the immature guys that were out there and I didn't want somebody else's cast-off baby— certainly not for my kids! I've dated one man exclusively, but there are almost 20 years between us, and that presents a problem for me. I don't want to be widowed at 50 or 55. I'm too unsettled to make a decision, so I'm not going to bother. There's no need to make a decision. We've helped each other along the way, and if nothing else that's been the best part of our relationship. It's been a mutually supportive situation. He's been wonderful to the children. They jump all over him when he's here, and he's here a lot. They've even spilled food on him. But then he's got a grandchild their age. And when I think about *that*, it stops me. Fatherhood is not easy for him again!"

If you decided to marry again, what kind of a person would you look for?

"We both must have a faith. That's a requirement of mine. I have to marry a Christian. But my friend comes to church only for my sake, so that's a real barrier. It's so hard to compromise with another human being, and if you don't have a common faith to start with, it's 90 percent against you! He's talking marriage but I get very nervous about it. He'll never push it, but I don't want to date him for 10 years and then look back and say, 'I could have had a home for my children, a family unit.' I want them to have some idea of a family. I don't want them to look into other people's windows.

"I don't have the energy to date other people. I tried it one night at a party, and I came home early. I hated it. These people couldn't talk to each other until they had several drinks, and I wondered what was wrong. They were half-married and half-unmarried. I don't want to go through that sleazy, singles scene. The only relationship left is this one, fulfilling and not demanding. We're comfortable together. I'm happy with the way it is, as long as nobody puts demands on me. And I don't feel guilty. I want to become a whole person, and I'm becoming me after 33 years of being—whoever!"

Marilyn's experience illustrates convincingly that happiness need not be born in marriage and killed by a divorce. With God's help she is beginning to get it together. Having a Christian philosophy of life gives her a positive outlook. She is struggling but she knows what she wants from life. She has set her goals and is determined to reach them!

5

Alexander Shares His Secrets of Success

Alexander has a philosophy for his home and he practices it. Alexander is a very together guy. He has had quite a while to adjust to being single again. His teenagers love him very much and emulate his warm, friendly ways.

Alexander received custody of his two teenagers when they chose to join him in his new home and surroundings. Part of the reason why Pete and Roz made the decision to travel halfway across the country was because their mother remarried, and they had some problems getting along with their new stepfamily. But the choice has turned out to be most beneficial because Alexander is an outstanding father.

But let Alexander talk for himself. "My home is one of a lot of responsibility. Responsible children don't need to be told and directed. They know, for instance, that there are certain things that have to be done in a household. We have divided all the chores.

"Responsibility has spilled over into other areas. For example they are as interested in my day as I am in theirs. They are concerned about my health. They make sure I jump rope and eat the proper foods."

Alexander believes in setting goals. "We are developing a five-year plan. They are working toward things they want to achieve. I try hard to get them to see the value in accomplishing things toward a goal each day, each week, each month. This does not mean the goal is cast in concrete. Should they decide to work in a different direction they will be flexible and change, but I try to keep them committed toward a direction. 'I want you to grow up well,' I tell them. 'I love you very much and I will always love you.' But I said, 'This is my home, and these are the things I have and these are the rules.' "

Many parents have not been so lucky in the area of communication. How do you accomplish this?

He chuckled. "Okay, fair question. This began when they were very small. Divorce is very tough on children and it took a long time before they could even begin to understand. But the good feelings the children and I had were still there. I worked on the continuing relationship. I kept in touch with them by long distance calls. The children said it seemed as though I was on a long vacation. When we got together, I knew we could pick up our relationship again, because we had an established base, a firm existing line of communication.

"I listen to every word they say. I listen to their friends when they come over. Their friends tell me things they do not share with their own parents. Teenagers often think someone else's parent is *safe*. The spontaneous part is what tells me the most! Ask the right kind of questions to get them started sharing."

Alexander is a high-energy person with a healthy, positive attitude toward life.

"If you are a person interested in life, not afraid of the competitive world out there, your kids will love to share in your activities. In their teen years their learning rate is very steep. If you say, 'I'm too tired, I just want to stay home,' or 'Let's watch television tonight' (for the umpteenth time) you will lose them.

"Generally children and teenagers are very proud of you and at times they want to be with you. Sometimes my daughter Roz and I go to the beach. We sit and watch the waves come up and go back out, listening to the sounds of the beach. This is what builds the relationship, even when you are quiet. They feel good. I don't mean I become their pal, but I share in these experiences that they will remember. The time you spend now can be part of the wisdom that helps to formulate their future decisions. I have learned a lot about my teenagers while shopping with them at the supermarket. They do not buy junk foods that could mess up their complexion. They read labels and their hands reach for the products that have the words *no preservatives*. It is amazing for me to see how interested they are, and the time they have spent studying in nutrition class. I know more about them from a shopping trip to the supermarket."

Alexander became more and more excited. "You can continue learning about your children by the books they read, the friends they have, the movies they want to see, the music they listen to, the people they want to get to know. If you do not like the direction they're taking, you have developed a fundamental base of communication. You can help them to change, if you feel this would be beneficial. Last night my son, who is in junior college, and I went out to dinner. His desire is to be on his own in a field where he can fulfill his potential. I gave him some direction and suggestions. Kids need the experience in making their own decisions. It is like telling them, 'Do not speed on the freeway.' Until they receive their first speeding ticket, they will not know what it is to go to court. If you've done it once, you usually don't want it to happen again!

"Right now I'm paying his expenses. With a B average he can continue to live here rent free, but if he should decide to go to work and not finish college, then he will pay me back for the college expenses. Peter can now fit into my clothes and he helps himself to my closet! He is terrific, always placing the clothing back, clean and brushed. For a long time he has done his own laundry and ironing."

Peter is a highly responsible young man. While attending college he holds down a part-time job and pays most of his expenses.

"Peter brought up the subject of productivity to me. I asked him what he was getting out of the movies, and the TV programs he was watching. What was he learning? His answers indicated that he really did not want to spend the time in non-productivity. You could waste your life in front of the tube and then ask yourself what happened? I suggested to Peter that he keep a record of his days for a week to see where he was spending his time. Also I strongly urged him to start some projects which could be completed in a few months."

What discipline guidelines have you set up for your family?

"The children have been with me since they were in their middle teens. The only discipline that has been effective is to take away privileges. No force. The key to disciplining is trying to reason with them. I start with the item of least importance and remove the privilege. I ask, 'Is this the person you want to be?' It helps to define their behavior and feelings. Peter has taken good care of himself because of his participation in sports. But Roz has an interest in smoking pot. We've had many discussions on the subject. I have asked, 'What is the purpose for smoking pot? What does it do for you? Do you go along with the crowd? Why do you need it?' I have told her, 'You are not a weak person. You do have confidence in yourself. You don't have to do it to be accepted.' I can't tell her to cut it off absolutely. She just turned 18. For *her* to make the decision would be best. She told me she doesn't do it often. I believe her. I remind her I am not asking her to be perfect!"

Alexander smiled. "When she is driving, for example, she has a very low tolerance for other people. If someone pulls out in front of her she beeps the horn quickly. She is beginning to be more moderate. There is no way to rush progress. We are very close, but I also know that these are signs of insecurity. That is also part of being a woman. This is the area where I need to chat with some of my friends who are also raising children without two parents; and I have friends who talk to Roz, woman to woman. Discipline has not been an unsolvable problem, but it has been frustrating to me at times. It's important while being patient with your children to steer between the tolerant indulgences of allowing them to get away with everything and the strict discipline which causes them to think you have turned into a harsh jailer. Disciplines must be adjusted to the ages of your children."

What do you do for yourself? Do the teenagers take up all your free time? And what about remarriage?

"Yes, they do take time." He drew a deep breath. "I

69

want to get married some day, but everything will have to be right. I would like to marry a woman who has outside interests and a life of her own. Sometimes I think the time I spend with my children has been a threat to women. Children will take 100 percent of your time if you let them. I said to them, 'I have my own life to live. My total aim in life is not to make you happy, although your lives are very important to me.' They want me to date, and they even look for me. I like to have them meet my date, and sometimes I take my children with me on a date."

Do you think you have over-compensated with your children?

"I hope I haven't. You always worry when a parent makes promises, 'If you will come and live with me I will do thus and so.' I asked Roz the other day, 'What would you like to have me do differently?' She said, 'You are raising me just the way I want to be raised.' Her grades this last semester fell short of a B average. Now she has lost some privileges, as per our agreement. She cannot drive my car. She has to take a bus to get to her part-time job. Upon occasion Roz and I will get going at one another and let off steam. We are human beings; I don't walk around holding it all in. It is not easy, and progress comes very slowly."

What about your spiritual life—God and religion?

"In my mind God and religion are very important." Alexander's response was quick and sure. "I have been very successful because of His guidance and help. Decisions I have made are not because of my intellect, but because He guided me into thinking that way. My children believe in God, although they are not attending a church school. They don't have a relationship with

Christ. Yes, you can say I am a born-again Christian. The other day Roz pointed to a church she would like to attend and we are making plans to go. Peter knows God has affected his life, the direction he has chosen, but he needs to develop more compassion."

What else has worked for you that might be beneficial to other parents?

"*Let young people talk about themselves,*" he suggested. "Listen to them clearly, thoroughly and completely. Listen lovingly. Be sure to hear their spontaneous, off-the-wall remarks. Think about what they say and try to see their point of view. Keep current. They change every six months or so. Find out where they are now.

"*Participate with them in whatever activities you can.* Do some things spontaneously with them. Experience new experiences. Arrange the activity and enjoy the participation. Let them plan and you join in with their plans too.

"*Ask them to list things they are interested in.* Build the relationship. Create the right atmosphere for love to grow. Good memories are very important. Get them to update the list every six months.

"*Another thing I do is to have them answer four questions.* I have written them down:

"(1) What are the three most important things you like best about me?

"(2) What are the three most important things you like least about me?

"(3) What one thing can I do now to improve my relationship with you?

"(4) What one thing do you think I would like you to do to improve our relationship?

"Be prepared for some negatives when you ask these

71

questions. They may be critical of you. Don't be uptight. Use your experience and your wisdom. Don't be over-bearing."

Alexander has creatively dealt with many issues and has successfully navigated through a difficult period with his teenagers. His example of a one-parent family illustrates that it is possible to make it.

Part III

Adjusting in a Stepfamily

6
Why Is It Hard to Live in a Stepfamily?

Building a single-parent family is tough, but adjusting to a stepfamily may be even tougher! Many parents are cautious because of the intricacies and problems of new relationships, but stepfamilies are still getting launched at an increasing pace.

In the sixties and seventies close to 60 percent of all divorcing people had children under 18. Many of these parents remarry. With one child under 18 the chances for a successful marriage are very good; with two children the chances are slightly less and with three children considerably less. Younger divorcees remarry sooner. Men and women in their forties and fifties take twice as long to remarry as those in their twenties and thirties; 50 percent of those who are divorced remarry in about three years, but 40 percent of those remarriages end in divorce.

One out of 14 couples has stepchildren. One out of

seven children in America under 18 is a stepchild! If the divorce rate continues to increase the number of step-children will be greater since a large percentage of people with children remarry. What is it like to live in a stepfamily? What could it be like if we really knew how to make it work?

Spiritual Implications of the Second Marriage

Even though the question is not within the scope of this book, something should be said about the spiritual ramifications of remarriage. We realize that this is a touchy matter in many Christian circles. Some Christians who are outspokenly against divorce under any circumstances are as vehement in their opposition to marrying for a second (and certainly never a third) time.

Doctrines, interpretations and viewpoints vary. Some churches refuse remarriage even if they allow divorce strictly on scriptural grounds. Other denominations allow remarriage only if the other partner was guilty of adultery or desertion and the one remarrying can prove innocence. Still others allow remarriage if there is repentance on the part of the person wanting to remarry. And there are a few who leave it to the individual's conscience without exerting pressures.

We realize that divorce and remarriage are facts to be dealt with. The Scriptures hold up the ideal of marriage, but they also present a loving, forgiving Saviour who talks about matters like divorce. When we seek guidance for such a question as this we should ask ourselves:

What is Jesus like?

What does He teach?

How did He live out the will of God?

What characterized His life?

Why did He clash so vehemently with the legalists of His day?

Do we hear in His teaching the notes of compassion and mercy?

Do we see in His life a sympathetic understanding of people and their problems?

If you are not satisfied in your own mind when you search the Scriptures for answers to the above questions, you may wish to consult an understanding pastor or Christian counselor.

Pressures on Stepmothers and Stepfathers

What's in a name? A stepparent can consider the "step" not as a step removed from parenthood (negative), but as a step to acceptance (positive). It isn't easy to approach being a stepparent in a positive way. There are many complications for the stepfamily. For example, husband number two must pay child support to wife number one which doesn't leave much for family number two. Wife number two may resent that she doesn't live as well as she formerly did. And husband number two needs to adjust to raising more children, possibly at a time in life when he thought he was through with all that. Or he may not have his own family and resents having to raise *hers*. How can he guide these children who may object to his role as head of the house and find it impossible to call him "Dad"?

In the meanwhile father number one may be holed up in some bachelor apartment. Occasionally he gets a visit from his kids, but he is thrust out of his home, very much alone in the world. He may even hear horror stories about the new stepdad.

Ginger, now 15, was 10 when her mother remarried. Ginger says of her stepfather: "It isn't a father-daughter relationship, because he doesn't treat me like a daughter. He makes remarks. He seems to think that I'm Marilyn Monroe or something. He treats me like a sex symbol. That gets on my nerves. He knows it bothers me. That's why he does it. He thinks it's funny. We don't have like a close relationship. I liked him at first but not anymore."

"I hated my stepfather," 13-year-old Elsie told us. "I tried to like him, but he didn't make any kind of a show of being a father. When I heard they were going to get married, I started crying. And I didn't know what he was like then. My stepfather picked on me. One time I was singing in the kitchen while doing the dishes. He said, 'Don't sing.' I talked back. He yelled at me. Sometimes he'd hit me. Then he'd say, 'Don't tell your mother, or you'll get in trouble.' When he was spanking he said if we moved our body one inch, he'd give us another one. I'm glad he's gone now. It's more peaceful. Mom and I get along good."

Pressures on stepparents can be great. One mother confessed: "I almost panicked when I realized I am now a stepparent!"

Why did she panic? Could it be the odious press stepmothers receive? In literature they're featured as wicked, selfish, jealous, uncaring creatures who specialize in victimizing children. And today's newspapers tell stories about stepparents who beat stepchildren, and stepchildren who shoot their stepparents.

"I froze when they called me stepmother. I am not a mother nor a stepmother, but I do know something about being a friend. Bill's sons call me Rhonda." Rhonda felt comfortable as a friend, and that was her choice to make. But it's not the same as parenthood.

Problems with Stepbrothers and Stepsisters

Not all problems are between stepparents and their stepchildren. Many families have not been able to make it because their children couldn't or wouldn't adjust to their new brothers and sisters. Because of their hostile, aggravating behavior, they were unable to live amid the intertwining relational problems of five, six, seven or eight—or more—people.

Bob and Dan are twins, 17-year-old surfers. Their father gained custody of all three of his boys.

"We had housekeepers who lived with us. We had several," said Bob who was seven when his parents divorced. "We sure got rid of them quick! We were just little brats, and nobody liked us and we caused a lot of mischief."

"Dad gave that up after a couple of years. And we took care of ourselves. Then he married Laura," Dan added.

"We were excited about this because she had a son who was about our age and we were good friends. We had him in Boy Scouts. We introduced his mom to my dad. She also had two smaller children," said Bob.

"But when we all moved together," continued Dan, "we didn't get along too good. Brothers and sisters fighting, you know. Sometimes our family against theirs. Somebody wants to watch one program on TV and somebody another. We had only one TV. Six kids. Wow!

"Dad had hassles with Laura too, but I think it's because of us kids that they got divorced after six months. We broke it up. We kept this house and we've been taking care of ourselves ever since."

"We didn't feel too bad about that divorce," added Bob, "because we didn't like Laura too much. She was very cranky, would make us work all the time, do mean stuff. She always favored her kids.

"I remember one problem when Dad was married to Laura. Laura said that Mom was to take all the kids for visitation, and Mom wanted us to come one at a time, so she could spend more time with us alone."

Dan explained, "We went one at a time to visit Mom, just like she asked. It was better that way. Mom doesn't like arguing."

"Yea, with just one of us with her we wouldn't argue. I don't always get along with my twin brother, but do other brothers?" concluded Bob.

Sometimes the problem of adjusting to stepfamilies is one of jealousy.

Fifteen-year-old Ginger says of her stepfamily, "I wanted sisters. I never had any, so here I got two—they came with the package—one a year younger, the other two years older. At first I thought, 'Wow, it's really going to be great. I have another dad and sisters.' But I still had that threat in there, you know, it won't be *my* mom any more, it will be *our* mom. *His* wife. That was very much of a threat. When my mom and dad have fights my grades go down. It's pretty much when I get upset about something that my grades will fall. Now I'm back working for A's. I'm pretty much of a hider when I get upset. I go in my room and nobody knows what's going on."

Children trapped in divorce are confused when one parent lives across town or in another city, while they must live in a new family and put up with stepbrothers and stepsisters and a stepparent. Do they really want to get along with all those strangers? Do they wonder where they belong and to whom they belong? Are they frightened because they're unable to figure out this crazy, mixed-up world? How do they tell their friends and teachers and people at church that Dad doesn't live at home anymore, or that they now have a new family?

Kitty is 16 and her younger sister, May, is 14. "Our first Christmas together was very hard," commented the pretty and bright Kitty. "Six kids! We had to get along.

They came to live with us 'cause their mom wouldn't keep them. And we only had three bedrooms. My sister May and I had to share a bedroom. We never had to do that before. At first we thought it would be fun. But it wasn't so much fun. We never had brothers or anything. Trying to get along with everybody, we didn't know how. They would tease us and pick fights. You know boys. And me and May had to clean the house. They never did anything."

"We'd fight and argue," said May. "And we'd say 'Shut up!' and 'You're not my brother.' None of my friends have a big family. I wasn't used to that."

"But it's changed a lot," continued Kitty. "We get along better. It wasn't easy on my mom and Robert either. One time I was doing the dishes and my mom was yelling at Robert, and I yelled at her so loud. I threw the dishes in the sink and ran upstairs to my room, and Mom just stood there. I yelled because I didn't want to see it happen again! Between her and Robert."

"Robert takes his boys places but he won't take us," May said. "They're the Josephsons and we're the McLeods. I felt really bad. It was just us before."

Decisions About Discipline and Responsibility

"How dare you spank my child when you allow yours to get away with everything?" Alicia's anger was not directed at the child but at her husband, the stepparent. The questions how, when and who does the disciplining need to be considered before the peace of the home is shattered. Finding the right methods for each family will vary with the ages of the children as well as their temperaments.

There are times to discipline, there are times not to discipline. When the household rules are broken and chores aren't done (and the children know what is ex-

81

pected) then discipline in eminent. Emotions can become raw for stepparents.

Dick was eight and his sister Shelly was four when their mother remarried. "I was happy that we had another father. When we came home from school there now were lots of kids. He had two sons and two daughters."

"We got along real good. I kind of wanted Mom to get married again," said Shelly. "I didn't like being alone."

"It was just hard for me to accept him. A new dad? But eventually I did. After about six months I called him 'Dad.' But he did some weird things you know."

"He would always hit us," Shelly added, "but he never hit his kids once the whole time they lived with us. We got spanked lots."

"It didn't happen to me as much as it did to Shelly," said Dick. "He thought she was being spoiled."

That marriage lasted eight years. When Dick was in the eleventh grade the families split up. "They would always go into the bedroom and we could hear them screaming. We didn't really know what the fights were all about."

"I was kind of happy that they split. I didn't blame myself. Things were not working out too good," explained Shelly.

Eileen and Richard were married in their late twenties, each having two children. They shared their struggles. "During the week the children got along fine with only minor scraps, but on the weekends when we entertained guests they created problems and fought." Eileen quickly corrected one situation with a swat to the rear end of the young child. Richard did not believe in spanking and chose to involve the child in a lengthy discussion while dinner was being delayed. Eileen was on edge. It was unfair to her guests.

82

When they came to grips with the real issues they realized the children were creating the opportunity for exclusive attention from Richard. "After the emotions drained away we could sit down and talk about the incidents. Then we began to see our approaches to discipline differed greatly." After the guests left they discussed the matter with the children. Now they're moving in unison. Conflicts stemming from unsolved discipline problems are a factor in the demise of second marriages.

There are times when our best response is not to discipline. "My former home was a place of chaos," Carol recalled. "When my first husband and I had a disagreement he expressed his anger by yelling. Then he backed the car rapidly down the driveway with the tires squealing. With Kevin my life is calmer, a more peaceful ebb and flow. I was beginning to feel like my own self. However, my two children in junior high became antagonistic and refused to do their chores. They complained that, 'The house is as quiet as a tomb. And we never go anywhere.' In comparing their dad to their stepfather they labeled their stepfather dull."

The children's stepfather hadn't been married before. He was confused by their attitude. Wisely the couple attended a family counseling center. With help from the counselor they saw that the children's behavior was the result of changes in their lives. In a short time the children had been expected to "come along" to what their mother considered a better life-style. In their new neighborhood there were no children their ages as in the old. They attended a new church and didn't like the kids.

Carol and Kevin asked the children to suggest some place they would like to go as a family once a month. This took the children by surprise. Since church was a drag they also visited other churches. After a year they joined a church in which they all could be happy. And problems of adjusting to responsibilities began to smooth out.

Struggles with the Reach-In Parent

"Everything seems to move along well. Then Jan's ex does something to reach in and cause a sonic boom in our home." Tony spoke with obvious annoyance. "When the two kids came back from spending Christmas, Jan and I stood in the doorway looking at them with unbelief. There they stood with their Christmas presents wiggling in their arms. Five-year-old Robbie said very defiantly: 'Look at the puppy. My Daddy said I'm old enough to raise a dog.' His older sister brought a puppy also. I would have liked to punch their father in the nose. The children know how Jan and I feel about pets," Tony continued. "And Jan has plenty to do with our new baby, without having to care for puppies. The baby is the bond to join our families together. It was hard but the next day we took the puppies back. Robbie cried and cried. Then we stopped at the pet store and bought fish."

"When the baby is older we may have dogs," Jan spoke calmly. The reach-in technique of parents without custody is difficult to deal with, hurts the children and causes the stepfather to play the role of the heavy. When the non-custody parent discovers his plans have backfired he sometimes gives up. Unfortunately some may be more stubborn.

Ruth has one child, a daughter who adores her father. "He is always months behind in his child support but when birthdays and holidays roll around he arrives on time with expensive presents."

"Sandy is only eight," Ralph complained. "He treats her as though she is a teenager. It is hard to know what to do, but we have stored the stereo and the tape deck in the attic!"

"The portable TV we exchanged for clothes and books and items she needs. However Sandy felt we were being cruel to her and she cried for her TV and her daddy."

Can parents and stepparents work together for the enrichment of each child, teaching worthwhile principles, and refrain from playing games even children don't wish to play?

Problems of Faith and Worship

Problems of faith may arise in the new family, but there can also be a new birth of faith.

"We would want to go to church and sometimes he'd say no. He wouldn't let us go," commented Harriet, a bright 14-year-old. "Maybe his daughter didn't want to go to church, so he just made everybody stay home. I have a lot of friends at church and that's fun. There are a lot of things the Lord has given us, though. We pray for things. My faith is stronger now. I depend on church lots more. I don't know why, but I do. I got to know the Lord better after my parents were separated. I've come to the reality that Jesus Christ is my Saviour. I'e got baptized too."

"When I was little we always went to church," Jean told us. Her secre family life was shattered when she was 12. "It was something we all did as a family. But when my family separated, I didn't go regularly anymore. The feeling just wasn't there. Mother worked hard, but she didn't go regularly. After a couple of years I got back on my own. When I was 16 I started teaching Sunday School. My Christian friends started taking me along with them. That all pulled it together for me."

Forming a new family is a challenge beset with dangers. But it is not a mission impossible. One couple confessed: "During the first year of our new family we did not experience *one peaceful day!*" The wife almost became unglued. Then Mary Ann added: "Our faith in God, perseverance and stubbornness saw us through."

Prayer and determination can bring success. Stepfamilies that have learned how to communicate their ideas and to express their feelings succeed. The secret is in listening and trying to understand each other.

7

There Is an Art to Stepparenting

"When my wife's oldest daughter introduced me to her friends as her stepdad," George related glowingly, "she gave me a look of love from her big, blue eyes. I will never forget that look and her short, but warm, hug as she went out with them. Now she's left the nest and if she ever needs help I find myself dropping everything and grabbing her mom and saying, 'Come on, MaryJo needs us!'"

"Mom, you're my only mother, and I will never call anyone else 'Mother' except you, but I like Dad's wife. She is teaching me how to make macrame wall hangings and I hope you don't mind if I spend some time over there."

As these testimonies indicate it is possible to have a happy, harmonious home where stepparents and stepchildren can live together. What is the secret to success? Is there a special combination of stepparents and stepchildren that works better than any others?

Various Combinations of Stepparents

Full time—This is the stepparent who has the step-children all the time with very little interruption.

"My new wife has custody of her children and they live with us. They are always underfoot. However, my job requires a great deal of travel and I can escape," grinned a new stepfather. Why does he need to escape?

One stepfather moaned, "Don't they know I am not a do-it-yourself man like their father? The pile of broken toys and things are stacked high. I don't know how to fix them."

"Honestly," a stepmother complained, "at every meal one of his children always, and I mean *always*, looks at the food on the table and groans, 'How gross.' Or, 'Why do you cook so weird?' Or, 'Why don't you ever cook something I like?' "

Part time—One month in the summer the children come to visit the parent who has what the courts call "reasonable visitation."

"The telephone rang continually," Carolyn, the step-mother admitted. "Their mother called long distance twice a day to see if they were okay. We had to be home or she would call the next day and scream, 'Don't you know I call at least two times each day and I want to know how they are?' Did she think we were going to burn them in a furnace or leave them in the woods?" Carolyn hopes next year, summer never comes.

The weekend warrior—A stepmother takes in her stepchildren like the weekly wash. Her own children are tidy and pleasant. His moppets, with soiled clothes and unwashed bodies, arrive like wild Indians. When the front door flies open their father reaches for his well-worn hat, shoulders his golfbag, throws a kiss in their direction and says, "Catch ya later, Honey." And step-mother is a frustrated baby-sitter.

One-day-every-other weekend—This day becomes one continuous lark for the kids with Dad in the role of the entertainer. Amusement parks, rides, thrills, spills and a glamorous restaurant to end the day, while stepmother gasps for breath and says, "This is *not* my cup of tea." If it isn't, why does she bother to go along?

Combination full-time, his-and-hers routine—This is a double feature with each parent starring in the role of parent and stepparent. Only the show never ends except for short intermissions when they can synchronize their exes to take all the children for a weekend. They need the break.

Sometimes it is easier to adjust to being a full-time stepparent than an infrequent one. How can stepparents cope with stepchildren they see only once in a while? How can they develop the art of stepparenting?

Avoid Being Indulgent

Often the stepparent feels that his/her own children are being neglected and require extra attention; or many stepparents who see their spouse's children infrequently think of themselves as friends who nurture and support. The degree of friendship is up to you, whatever you feel is appropriate. But do not lavish the children with expensive gifts. Buying and doing are not the same!

Don't try to win their affection by being permissive. If bedtime is 8:30 in their home, keep the routine. Look at it from the other side. Miranda complained, "It takes me two or three days to get the children regulated after they spend a weekend with their father and his new wife. They stay up late, eat junk food, watch TV, and when they come home I reach for the aspirin."

Find a Neutral Home

It is wise to select a new place to live, or else you may

hear from your children: "My father's new wife is an invader! She uses all my mother's dishes and stuff."

"Every time I see my stepfather I think he doesn't belong here," Bryan said. "He is an intruder."

Remember the twins we spoke of in the last chapter—Bob and Dan? Their father decided to marry a third time. About two years ago he married a woman with three sons. They have a unique arrangement: both families live in their own homes.

"This house isn't big enough for six kids. When we were with Laura, at one time five of us boys were in one room on bunk beds. That was mean," Dan explained.

"Now we see our stepbrothers on weekends or when they come over or we go over," said Bob. "It's not like they're our real brothers. We see them less than we see our friends at school."

"I like my stepbrothers. They're really cool," Dan said.

This is an unusual situation, but it seems to be working for them!

Allow Freedom of Speech

Some children cannot face the pain of divorce. The divorce, remarriage, visitations with the other parent all take their toll. Even after a number of years in a stepfamily they may still long for the original family. They may desperately want to know their real father or mother. Not all children look like they hurt; children who act normal may be covering their hurts by good behavior, but inside they may be suffering. They need to find a path to reality and security.

Sometimes on holidays children become moody because they need both parents for security. Fantasy can become a part of their daily agenda. Parents need to spend special times each day with children who live in a world of fantasy. They need to let the children talk about their fantasies. Allowing them freedom of speech will help children who hurt learn to adjust.

Children have hidden agendas and unspoken expectations. You need to gain their confidence so that they will learn to talk freely. They listen carefully to what they want to hear, and when you talk about something close to where they are now, they pick up their antennas and tune in. When they gain confidence in you, then they may begin to express their expectations, hostilities and broken dreams.

Don't expect overnight changes even if you've taken time with them. That's par for the course. Effective stepparenting takes time.

"When Dad first met Evie I didn't get along with her," 15-year-old Marsha confided. "We really fought. And with her son too. He's a year younger. After they got married we really didn't get along for about a year. She'd tell me what to do, and I wouldn't do it. I told her: 'You're not my mom. I don't have to listen to you.' I didn't respect her in any way. But now she's like a sister to me. Her and I are best friends. We talk about everything."

Evie gained Marsha's respect and confidence by listening to her needs. Now they both enjoy a bond of friendship.

Allowing freedom of speech, however, doesn't mean your home must be a vocal battleground.

Create a Peaceful, Serene Environment

"I can be very difficult," volunteered Kitty freely. "I used to be able to talk to my mom, but now when she raises her voice, I raise my voice and I can shout louder."

"When they get into a fight," added May, "Mom just

goes, 'Why don't you go live with your dad?' "

"I resent that. I resent that very much." Now Kitty was crying. "I don't think that's right, because she says she loves me and then she wants to kick me out. That's the way it comes across to me." She was sobbing.

"But it hasn't happened for a few months," added May tearfully, trying to calm her sister.

"I never used to be aggressive. I was very quiet. Until Mom got remarried. Then I had to start speaking up for myself. Or I would have nothing at all. My mother is a very aggressive woman. That's why I'm aggressive, I think."

Your life-style creates stability for the home. It becomes a continuing discussion of the principles upon which your lives are built. Long after the children leave the nest, your Christian way of life will continue to show itself in them and in you.

Steve and Margie wrote a short description of the atmosphere they desired for their home and posted it on their refrigerator. "Our home is a place for renewal, peace, harmony, joy, learning and growth." The children were encouraged to express their interpretation of the meaning of the words.

Vern and Juliette and their children were one big, happy family for three months. Then Vern declared that coming home was just as though he had stepped into a war zone. Juliette looked disheartened and miserable amid the noise and confusion. Vern came across a saying of unknown origin: "Noise is pollution to the soul, but quietness and serenity are to govern our lives." As an outgrowth of discussions with the children (although the children were reluctant) all noisy games, fighting, chasing through the house ceased one-half hour before father came home. For the balance of the evening quieter activity was called for. As a direct result Juliette's

92

second child who was the pivotal force behind the aggravation and noise developed an interest in reading magazines from his stepfather's trade. That led to creating gadgets in the garage together. End of the war!

Bill and Wanda told us how they concentrated on one rule of conduct: no one walks into a room talking or screaming to gain attention. No interrupting. Sounds simple?

"Bill's kids were driving me up the wall," Wanda admitted. "They could do three things well—talk, talk and talk." Wanda's two children were quite gentle. In a short while the two aggressive ones had taken over. One of Wanda's girls said, "Mother, it was not this bad when you and Dad used to fight before you divorced!" When Wanda passed those comments on to Bill he paid attention to her complaints.

When a couple works on a problem, not making excuses for their own siblings, positive action can benefit all. Quickly the children test and push against the rules to find out exactly where the fences are, but fences only stay intact when both parents support each other. Children eventually work with the program when they discover Mom and Dad operate in harmony.

Don't Compete with Natural Parents

Never try to eradicate or do anything that could be damaging to the character of the natural parent. Each child has a set of parents, living or dead, and they deserve that world untampered. A stepparent would be wise not to come between the child and the biological parent, nor to take away from the existing relationship. To achieve a healthy balance is not always easy. Be your own person, and be supportive of your mate in his or her role of parenting. But, do not compete with the natural parent. Be moderate. Be yourself. Be considerate.

Give Your Spouse Equal Time

One ingenious stepparent shared her unique plan. "Every night when Barry returns home from work I join him in the living room for an invisible time. When we sit in two special chairs, for all intents and purposes, we have turned invisible. If the children burst into the room and see us sitting there they turn around and leave. Sometimes they say, 'Excuse me.' We were determined before we brought our two families together under one roof that this was going to work for us! One day Jill and two of her girlfriends came into the room. Jill obviously wanted to ask us something. Turning around she said to her friends, 'My parents are not here.' Her friends said, 'What do you mean they are not here? I just saw them.' Jill answered, 'No you didn't.' She was so serious!"

You need time alone to survive. Romantic time, yes, looking fondly into each other's eyes over a white table-cloth with a candle flickering and soft violin music.

Stepparents Can Make It

A father of three young children moved in with a mother of three. They were sure it was going to last forever. The marriage lasted three months. A father with his two teenagers moved in with a mother of two. They lasted for two stormy years. Many factors in merged families can account for success or failure: the ages of the children; the blending of personalities; but the most important is the emotional maturity of the stepparents. Much will depend upon their ability to be flexible and to persevere. They are the pivotal force.

Stepfathers may turn out to be a real benefit to the new family:

"I've always been afraid of my father, ever since I was little. He'd slam the door when he came home," confessed Cara. "The whole house would vibrate. I'd go, 'Oh, no. He's home.' And I'd hide in my room. Anytime he went out I was so happy he was gone. I've always been afraid of him. If he got mad, he hit us. I remember a couple of bloody noses, because he had a big Mason ring."

"My stepdad has become my dad. He's more my father than my real father," said Ann. "My mom became a Christian just this past summer, and that's because I became a Christian before that. I was the first in my family. My stepdad has accepted Christ too and he'll ask questions. My real father is too stubborn, but I try to tell him."

"My stepdad is really a terrific person," said Joe. "He doesn't spend his money foolishly, and he wants to give my mother things she's never had."

"I have special feelings toward my stepfather too," announced Carl. "I was about 10 when he married Mom. I realize that the Lord allowed the divorce to happen. At the time I didn't. I didn't have a spiritual interpretation. But now I view my stepfather as my spiritual father, my teacher and counselor. My mom and my stepfather both came to know the Lord at the time of their marriage, and they've both been growing tremendously! My stepfather is *a gift from God*."

Guidelines for Building a Happy, Harmonious Stepfamily

In merged families, once goals have been set and everyone accepts them, the kids will begin to think, "We are one family." They are no longer separate compartments sandwiched into space, waiting for the first opportunity to split. Our study has shown, and national statistics indicate, that stepparenting is *not* always successful. But you can claim the blessing of a Christian household. By living the Christian life you will move from the authority you may have to the respect and love you will earn. Plant seeds of kindness, patience and understanding. They will grow.

Get to know other families who are stepparenting. Churches are a good place to meet them. *Comfort and encourage your hearts and strengthen them—make them steadfast and keep them unswerving—in every good work and word* (2 Thess. 2:17, *Amp*).

If things continue to be rough in the family after a few months, get help. Look for family counseling centers affiliated with churches. Invest time and money in counseling before problems gain a full head of steam.

In the meanwhile the following questions may prove to be very helpful!

1. Have I had time to heal from my previous marriage?
2. Am I a victim of my past? Can I put the past behind me?
3. Am I ready to face new problems, or do I think I have too many problems of my own?
4. If I am bitter toward my past mate what am I doing about it?
5. What are my objectives in the relationship with my stepchildren?
6. I have not been a parent before. How do I want to relate to my stepchildren and them to me?
7. I am a parent and enjoy my own children. How will I be fair with my stepchildren?
8. Can I look objectively at each child and think of them as individuals and not a package deal?
9. If I must talk in the presence of children about my ex-mate, will I say something positive?

10. Can I laugh at myself?
11. Can I share?
12. Do I think it is possible to be a positive stepparent when I don't feel good about myself?
13. If my stepchildren have been kept in the dark about their parents' divorce and they come to me for more information, will I:
    a. answer their questions?
    b. listen but defer the question to their parent?
    c. make excuses for each parent?
    d. fail to develop a relationship so I don't get asked tough questions?
14. Am I a good listener?
15. Am I concerned about forming good relationships?
16. How will I handle our cultural, educational and religious differences?
17. Instead of his or her traditions can I help develop our own as a family?
18. Can I and my mate agree on what behavior patterns need to change in a child? And how?
19. Will I be consistent?
20. Will I accept the responsibility of:
    a. setting a good example?
    b. sharing spiritual values?
    c. attending church and Sunday School?
    d. allowing for individual freedom?
21. How will I proceed concerning legal adoption and name changes?

Part IV

Pulling It All Together

8
We Can Help the Children of Divorce

Throughout this book we've listened to the voices of the children of divorce. We've looked at the single-parent family and how to have a stepfamily. Let's sum up in this last part what you can do to help the children of divorce, and what teenagers can do to help themselves.

Are you willing to become the one person who will stand in the emotional gap? In all probability you are the *best* person because you are the closest to your child. Your children need to talk to someone and that someone could be you. Are you able to take time out of your busy life to hear their woes objectively and without judgment? This requires skill, humility, patience, maturity and love. In order to become that concerned parent you must get your own act together, as we have previously shown.

The following 10 suggestions are a summary of what you may be able to do to help children of divorce.

Become Aware

Start by tuning into your children's lives, feelings and thoughts. Listen to them. Hear what they are saying in both their spoken and unspoken messages. Learn what is playing in the theatre of their lives. Be understanding.

When you're tuned in to your children you're making inroads. They will realize you really care, and they will learn to trust you more.

"Mom pushed me at first. I'd come home and she'd question me about my visits with Dad," Claudia told us. "I didn't like that at all. Finally I sat her down and said, 'Mom I don't want you asking me questions. I don't want to feel like I'm on trial.' She hasn't questioned me since. And because she hasn't I've seen him more. I also volunteer what we talk about, but I'm no messenger."

Try not to superimpose your ideas on what you believe they're experiencing. You may want them to think as you think, to see things as you see them, to express feelings similar to your own. You may have read somewhere about how they *should be* feeling, or you've heard other parents talk about their children and you may be tempted to transfer other children's feelings to your own. Don't fall into that trap. They are their own persons.

Since every person is unique and since every relationship is unique, no two people will behave exactly alike. Children may have some common characteristics, but we cannot mold them into our prepackaged ideal, expecting them to react according to predetermined patterns.

Accept what you hear and see and feel. When you become aware you help your children through trials.

Clarify the Issues

Undoubtedly they will be, for a time, in a state of confusion. So will you. Often with a change of values there follows an upheaval of their security and a loosening of a foundation, so that young children as well as teenagers will become perplexed for a while. They may not always express this through questions, but they're surely wondering what has happened to their family. What can they hold onto? Where are their lives moving now?

The time has come to clarify the issues, to answer their questions, to speak the truth honestly. It is necessary to temper this to the age of the child. Just as you do not tell a four-year-old all the details of human reproduction but only as much as he can absorb, so you can share the facts of your family upheaval. As children grow into their teens they will request more information and you will be more specific.

Explain the best you can what has happened to your marriage. Talk about yourself. Talk about the issues. Do it without malice, without undercutting remarks that attack the masculinity or feminity of the absent parent, without accusations and unnecessary judgments. Keep to the facts. You don't have to explain everything about finances or sex. Children are unable to grasp the total complexity, but the overall picture can be made clear.

A nine-year-old shared a dream with her mother: "Sometimes I dream that I have a father and he plays a bunch of games with me, and then one day, I forget what it was, but Mom kicked him out. And I'm sitting there and my eyes are popping out and she's going, 'You get out of this house.' And then I wake up."

Her mother interpreted the dream and helped her daughter to accept the fact that she had a dad who very, very seldom made contact with her.

101

Clarification will help your child to deal with his inner turmoil. Encourage him to express himself freely and help him to understand himself. When a child or teenager refuses to talk about his or her inward frustrations he is beginning to internalize. You can help him express himself by suggesting that you have some understanding of what he is feeling. You can say, "Perhaps you're feeling this way . . . and I understand." He may answer, "Yes, I do feel that way." Or he may disagree. Then you can ask why.

Stay away from put-down phrases like, "By now you should be able to cope." Give no absolutes like, "This is the way it is." Remain positive. Point the way to self-understanding. Keep in mind that divorce is tough on their self-image. You do not want the divorce to become a stumbling block in their path to coping with life later on.

Comfort

The need for comfort is universal. We need so much consolation for ourselves. We all readily accept compassion when it is sincerely given. We feel good when somebody understands us and communicates understanding.

Children are the same. In spite of the tantrums they throw occasionally, the rebellious moods they slip into, the times they withdraw to their rooms silently, their need for comfort remains constant. Perhaps their bizarre behavior is calculated to gain attention! Divorce is a total change for children and an adjustment for them to make. They don't have anything else with which to compare it. Comfort them by word and touch; tuck them in and kiss them goodnight and give them some good feelings.

Your teenagers will appreciate a hug. You can comfort them with kind, encouraging words, a special dessert, taking them places as a favor, or by giving them a listening ear when they're sharing their interests.

Perhaps it's unfair to place this burden on you just now. At other times you can give of yourself. Now you have need of someone who will reach out to you. You need comfort and understanding yourself. You'd like to have some cuddling and loving. The person with whom you have shared many years no longer lives with you. How can you give when you need to receive?

Are you preoccupied with yourself? Are you conscious of being a needy person? If in your grief you're able to release yourself and comfort others, especially your needy children, then in comforting others you yourself will be comforted! *Experience shows that the more we share in Christ's immeasurable suffering the more we are able to give of his encouragement. This means that if we experience trouble it is for your comfort and spiritual protection* (2 Cor. 1:5,6 *Phillips*).

Children of divorce need much affection and loving care. They may not tell you, but you will be able to sense it. When they experience your compassion, time will heal their wounds. Keep it up. Show them the love that has been extended to you from the Lord. Don't hold back. Then both you and your children will become winners over crisis!

Encourage Them

We humans need encouragement as well as comfort. Encouraging the children of divorce to keep on doing well, not to let down in their schoolwork, helping them set and achieve their goals, and accepting their failures without faultfinding is a great art. Give them positive input liberally.

But what if they bring home poor grades just when

they could be improving? Can you be understanding and not condemning? Can you point out why they may be failing some courses? Has the frustration and upset in their family contributed to their confusion? Encourage them to overcome frustrations. Since they have done well in the past, they will again be capable of good work now. Your encouragement will get them over rough places quicker.

Children readily recall that the family enjoyed good times you shared together but now experience no more. Children may become overly concerned with the past. Encourage them to look to the future. Help them to believe in your future together. Give them *hope.*

With personal encouragement for a child who flounders, you affirm: "No matter what, I accept you the way you are. I'll always love you. I may not approve of everything you do, but you can count on me and my love for you."

In reading this book you heard several children of divorce talk about self-doubt. They wondered why their parents didn't make it. They secretly asked themselves whether it could have been their fault. They were concerned about any rejection they received from one or both of their parents.

A parent needs to break through to the inner child. Children are real persons. They are worthy of all the encouragement you can give them. Acceptance is a great encouragement. And to parents of teenagers, if you see glaring negatives in your teenagr, there are positives. Look for them. You will find them. Begin by calling attention there.

Continue to Be Patient
After having listened and shown compassion and you still feel you're not getting through, don't give up. Be

patient! Endure! Continue! These words sound tough and you may be disillusioned. You have many extra pressures on you from your job, you have the care of the house and family, the details your spouse used to take care of, not to mention added responsibilities that now rest on your shoulders, and now you're asked to be patient as well? To endure more? Yes, it takes patience and perseverance.

The kids sure know how to test you. Do you think they may be doing it deliberately? Not necessarily. They know you're having a hard time but kids are kids. That's just the way they act when your patience wears thin. You may be absolutely convinced they're making trouble on purpose. Well, they're not. You're so on edge it only *seems* that way. They're preoccupied with their own pain and, as hard as this may sound, you need a big dose of patience to see you through. You will reap the reward of your labors in time. Trust God, believe in yourself and progress will come.

Learning patience and perseverance is like teaching a three-year-old to kick a soccer ball to his friend. He looks at the ball in his hands a long time. He just stands there. Then he takes a step forward. He still holds the ball. He waits again for several seconds. He starts to shuffle his feet, but he can't bring his leg up to meet the ball. So he takes another step forward. Again he stands there, concentrating on the ball, shuffling his feet. Then he takes another step forward. This time he shakes his head from side to side and says, "No." He doesn't want to part with the ball, and he doesn't want to risk lifting up his leg and possibly lose his balance.

Then the process starts all over again. He walks back a few steps, holding the ball, looking at it. He takes a step forward, stops, looks, shuffles his feet, hesitates, takes another step forward, stops. ... And again he turns around after several attempts and shakes his head from side to side. It goes on for a long time. His friend just waits and waits. He is very patient. He doesn't chide the boy for holding onto the ball for so long. He is a little older. He just walks around, waiting and watching his friend.

Finally the big moment arrives. After numerous hesitations the leg shoots up and meets the ball as he kicks it over his friend's head. The little boy then throws himself on the grass and rolls and tumbles, totally satisfied with his accomplishment. He rollicks with laughter!

To a bystander, kicking the ball looks like such a simple act, but for the three-year-old it is a major accomplishment. For any child to overcome a fear that he holds in his hands and doesn't know how to kick away, may take a long and difficult effort. If we can stand there encouraging him, loving him, waiting patiently for him, but expecting him to resolve his own conflicts, he may eventually gain the courage to kick his problems away.

Recognize Their Emotions and Share Your Own

Many parents label their children's behavior *Negative*. "They're miserable kids, they're disobedient, they're impossible!" The moment we attach these negative labels we limit our children not only in our minds but in theirs. If we call a child slow or lazy, we may see him only as slow or lazy and he may believe it too! Then we fail to accept the true child.

For example we may say, "Our daughter is withdrawn. She closets herself in her room. She barely speaks." Why does this girl have such a need for privacy? Why does she have to work out her own emotions? Does she need to find acceptance for what she is enduring? Aren't the chances greater that she will emerge out of her shell if she is consoled and shown acceptance?

Another child becomes overly aggressive. He releases his hostility almost constantly. He destroys and breaks things. He has extreme explosions of anger.

His inner anger needs to be clarified for him: "Do you know why you are angry?"

It needs to be understood: "Of course you are angry. You have good reasons to be."

It needs to be dealt with: "You can overcome your anger; you won't always be like this."

He needs to be ministered to: "I get angry too. I know how it feels."

Above all, he needs to be accepted: "It's okay to express your anger, but you don't have to become so destructive." The Bible says, *Be angry, and yet do not sin* (Eph. 4:26, *NASB*).

If a parent reacts to hostility with hostility, a cycle is set into motion. Refuse to allow yourself to be sucked into such a cycle. You need to break the cycle by penetrating to the source of anger in the child. That will bring about the healing of the emotions.

Feelings and emotions are valid. Share your own, but tailor them to the ages of the children. When your child or teenager rejects your vulnerability, you'd better stop. There's no point bleeding while you're being stomped on! When teenagers are unable to accept your sincerity, it's because they are still unable to handle themselves, just as a small child cannot understand why you're crying more these days. Some teenagers may be unprepared for too much honesty. So you'll have to go slower. Test the water.

Keep the Faith

Are you discouraged? Do you blame God for your divorce? Why didn't life work out better for you? Why do you have to face life anew in your twenties, thirties, forties or fifties? Why did God allow this to happen to you? Why didn't your marriage succeed since you are a Christian? Perhaps you were married to a Christian as well.

Whatever the reasons, you may be questioning your faith. Was all the time and effort you have given to the Lord and the church worthwhile? Why did it end like this? When you're questioning and confused, you send waves of doubt in the direction of your children. You may not openly ask these questions, but when you feel let-down and walk around stoop-shouldered, when worship becomes burdensome in your already overloaded week, you certainly influence your children.

Don't change your religious patterns now! If you have been in the habit of attending church and taking the children to Sunday School, keep it up. This is not the time to pull up roots. Your family needs consistency. Families and teenagers can find a new dynamic in Christian fellowship. In times of crisis they draw closer to God. They receive helpful answers as they search the Scriptures and in the presence of caring Christians they feel more secure. This is how healing of the emotions occurs.

Maybe your children toss questions in your direction. Why did God allow this to happen? Where is God now? Doesn't He care about us anymore? Why did He let Daddy (or Mommy) leave? Attempt to answer each question as best you can. Be honest and pray for answers. If you don't know an answer it's okay to say, "I don't know." Tell the truth. You can encourage them to talk to their Sunday School teacher or the pastor. The important point is that your faith will encourage their faith!

Continue good habits. If you're in the habit of saying prayers at night with your children, continue to pray with them. If you've been holding family devotions, don't stop. Offering prayers of thanksgiving before meals need not end. If a teenager becomes uncomfortable about family devotions or prayers at night, talk about it. Do not give up your own faith in the process. Though teenagers may balk, young children will follow. In any case let your family know you will remain steady in your beliefs. Your faith in Christ will never be in doubt.

Take Time for Family Fun

Your family needs time out. Even a mini-vacation is better than none. Outings, trips, vacations—you and your children need to look forward to these. Maybe you cannot travel as extensively or expensively as you're used to. But you can do things together as a family that cost little. Talk to the children honestly about money. Some families set aside one week in the summer to visit inexpensive places of interest. Beaches, mountains, parks, picnics, museums, and school sports are still very reasonable. Some are free. And it's being together and doing things together that counts. Build good memories.

You're still a family even though one member of that family is no longer at home. Perhaps you're able to include other family members who will join your outings occasionally, like grandparents, uncles, aunts, cousins, nephews and nieces. Some grandparents are happy to fly their grandchildren across the country for a visit. Not only will these times give your children a continued sense of family ties, they may become opportunities for enlarging their vision of the family, and as a result they will feel more secure!

Measure Responsibility

Changes have already occurred in your situation. If

you're a father who is taking care of your children, you've discovered the added responsibilities of cleaning the house, with such goodies as scrubbing the shower, the toilet and the oven, doing the shopping, the cooking, the washing and just about everything else. It is only natural to have your children help you. Give them as many responsibilities as possible so they will share the burden. Stretch them. Let them develop new skills.

If you're a mother who has custody and now are working, time will be at a premium for you. You have the added responsibilities of fixing things around the house as well as yard work. Let the family work together on weekends. Don't overload them. Be careful! We abolished child labor some years ago in this country! Miracles will happen with a we'll-all-pitch-in-and-do-it-together attitude. Remain sensitive to your children. Some are very willing to pitch in and help; they're eager and ready. They may even volunteer for certain tasks they enjoy doing, and if it sounds reasonable enough let them try things like cooking. Such ventures allow them to gain valuable experience, and they will develop self-reliance early.

Eighteen-year-old Art told us: "We kids were on our own. We didn't need a baby-sitter. We were in charge. We learned to cook and clean. I can do my own wash, wash dishes, clean the house and a lot of stuff that most of my friends never do. We do most of the work now. When Mom comes home from work, dinner is ready."

But what if you encounter a severe dose of rebellion from your teenager? You would think that the older they become the more helpful they will be. You may be wrong. It doesn't always work out that way. Don't mention the girl down the block who helps her mother all the time, since your teenager will bluntly reply that she doesn't like to be compared. When, however, they have helped you, thank and praise them for the job they did. You are grateful; let them know you are.

Above all you do not want to alienate your children. So, don't push them too hard. *To be overly demanding and lose the relationship is not worth it!* Lessen the load but do not remove all responsibility. Help your child to face pressure situations. In most instances understanding and acceptance is the best path to follow.

Let Everything Be Done in Love

Faith, hope and love. But the greatest of them is love (1 Cor. 13:13, *Phillips*). The suggestions we make to help the children of divorce can be summed up in one word—love. *Let everything that you do be done in love* (1 Cor. 16:14, *Phillips*). We suggest that you and your family read again 1 Corinthians 13. This chapter may be the best experience to guide your family into the way of love.

Surely you have many concerns. Your children create additional pressure for you. Your desire is to relieve them of their hurt and pain as much as you can. You want them to cope with life. So, raise some simple and helpful questions for yourself:

What is the loving thing to do in our situation?

What do my children need from me?

How can I best reach my children?

How can I help them? What are their needs?

What encouragement do they need from me?

How can my actions be guided by kindness and understanding?

How am I to discipline in love?

How can I allow them the freedom to become true persons?

How can I become more comforting and compassionate?

What does it mean for me to act as a loving person? Taking Christianity into everyday life is the supreme challenge for every Christian. But Jesus asks nothing less of us. One hour of worship per week is simply not enough. You can adopt a holy attitude for a short while, but how do you live out that faith you profess in church?

Our children live with us, watch us, scrutinize us, evaluate us and forgive us. But if we profess one thing and live another they will be the first to reject our faith and us!

Most of us want to live out our faith. We want to do the loving thing, we want to be kind, understanding and compassionate. How is it possible? All Christians receive the Holy Spirit when they are born anew. The Spirit is given for the express purpose of helping us to live our Christian lives. Reach out to God. Let His Spirit live in you daily, even hourly, always. If we are not aware of His presence, the fault lies not in the Spirit but in us. Living in the Spirit is never easy but it is possible. The more we acknowledge our need for God the more we rely on Him. The Kingdom of God belongs to the humble. And they find the loving way.

Life is not easy, but with God all things are possible. Allow His love to permeate your life and that of your children.

9
Teenagers Can
Help Themselves

P arents are pretty much responsible for helping young
children. But teenagers have to bear some of the burden
of recovering from the effects of divorce in their families. So now it's time to give this book to your teenager
to read, and especially this chapter.

As a teenager you face some strange new situations in
a single-parent family, or in a stepfamily. Your foundation has been shaken. You may not feel as secure as you
did when your family was still together. Now you're
challenged to live out the failure of your family.

Find Someone to Talk To

Perhaps you don't want to talk to other people about
your mixed-up feelings, but your insides feel like scram-
bled eggs. Do you wonder if there's someone somewhere who can really understand what you're going
through? Do you know other kids who have endured
their parents' divorce?

"I felt an emptiness inside, like something was taken
away from me," confessed Art. "I felt that it was my

113

fault that the divorce happened. I asked my brothers about that, and they felt like that too. I went through a lot of problems in junior high. That was because I had those problems at home, the divorce. They were the worst years I ever had."

Millie is now 19. Her parents divorced when she was a senior in high school, but the family turmoil had been severe for five years: "The marriage wasn't very good. It made me feel like I didn't even want to be around. Fighting all the time, or they weren't talking at all! One night I really got upset and left. That's the worst night I can remember. I just left for a couple of hours, not overnight or anything. I had a feeling it would happen. You always hear about other people being divorced, but you don't think about your own parents. Like my friends would say, 'Your parents are getting a divorce?' I'd say, 'Yes.' They'd say, 'That's too bad.' No it isn't really. It's not that bad. I thought it was for the best. At first I was upset and confused. But then it didn't faze me that much."

"My parents had been married almost 25 years," submitted Sherry who was in her late teens. "I blamed myself a lot, not knowing why. They went through two other kids without divorcing and then here comes me and they get a divorce! I did blame myself. Maybe I still do a little. It's hard to live through the ages of 13, 14, 15. That's a really self-incriminating age anyway, and then to have a divorce? For me it shook everything up that I believed in. The more difficult I became, the more I felt guilty."

Can you relate to these kids? Has your world fallen apart? Do you find it hard to understand why your father and mother can no longer live together? Are you angry about it? Do you wonder if some of their troubles were your fault? Are you feeling guilty? Abandoned?

Rejected? Has someone said to you: "You know, you haven't helped the situation by your behavior"?

Perhaps you're wondering what will happen to you and your family now? You're full of questions you're afraid to ask.

Yes, you're experiencing a lot of turmoil. That's normal. Begin to accept your feelings. One way toward acceptance is to sit down and talk with someone you can trust. Someone will understand you and bring you relief.

"I was upset being away from my father." Suzy spoke with emotion in her voice. "More than anything I was ashamed. Ashamed of living in that crummy place, and ashamed of my parents being split up. I didn't tell a soul. One day in class I had a kind of breakdown. The teacher kept me after class and I told him the whole thing. He became my confidant. Every day I went to him. He took a real interest in me. If he hadn't been there, I don't know what I might have done."

In time the parent you're with will be able to help you when you reveal your feelings, and possibly so will the parent who has visitation rights. This will depend on the kind of people they are. Perhaps both of them will listen to you and show you understanding. As they are able to overcome their own pain, they will be more free! They hurt and you hurt, and that means a tough time for everybody.

It's important to accept your feelings. Allow them to surface. The sooner you admit them, the sooner you can get your bearings. Once you understand the reasons why you feel the way you do and accept your right to feel this way, then you will be able to face the changes in your life.

Refuse to Take the Blame

Jerry blamed himself: "The first time my father had

a nervous breakdown, we kids were in the room fighting and my dad got really angry, and my mom came in and tried to stop it, and my dad hit my mom and I felt that it was my fault. I just had a lot of problems feeling my self-worth when I was growing up. Whether that was the divorce or not, I don't know. I think it probably was. But I don't feel guilty anymore. Maybe my middle brother went with my father because he's still working that through."

Many children and teenagers blame themselves for their parents' divorce. They believe if they had only been easier to get along with or behaved more like their parents wanted them to, the separation would not have occurred.

The tendency to blame yourself is natural. You may indeed have agitated the situation and upset your parents. Perhaps occasionally your parents fought about ways to discipline or control you. Perhaps one of them even told you if you had behaved better they would not have split up. Did someone lay a guilt trip on you for their inability to make it together? And do you agree with their evaluation?

Don't accept the guilt! They are responsible adults. They are individuals who are accountable for their own actions. You are not responsible for *their* marriage. As adults they need to assume responsibility for their own lives. It's not up to you to carry the blame. The sooner you throw off that guilt, the happier you will be. Your parents did not separate because of you! They divorced because one of them (or perhaps both of them) made that decision. Refuse to attach any fault to yourself.

If you have trouble doing this, remember that the gospel of Jesus Christ offers complete forgiveness for all our sin, for all our guilt, for everything. Jesus died for your sins. Everyone who comes to Jesus will be received, no matter what we may have done. God's grace is greater than our sins. Grace wipes all our sins away. We can be cleansed from all our guilt.

Don't Take Sides or Try to "Get Even"

"Don't take sides like I did," Kay stated. "I was so angry that in the beginning I didn't want to see my dad. He used to write me. I didn't answer. For about a year I didn't answer him or see him. When the divorce was over and he got married and this was the way life was going to be, then I was able to see him. We started to have lunches together. He asked me to his wedding, but I didn't go. I told him I couldn't handle that."

"Right after the separation we moved from a house into this apartment. Things got tight," Sara related. "The whole divorce was kind of a prolonged hurt. I had a hard time coping with my anger. I used to throw things, but I don't anymore. I grew out of that finally."

It's only natural for you to feel angry. You may want to retaliate, to get even for all the hurt you're experiencing. Is that why you're upsetting the home? But you may be doing it unconsciously. You really hurt so badly. You're becoming very hostile. And you probably believe that no one understands you.

How about admitting to yourself that you hurt? How about persuading yourself that you can make it? How about thinking of others instead of yourself? How about asking God for help? You *can* make it. You can be in charge of your actions. You can control yourself.

Sometimes teenagers retaliate against the parent who has left the home. They refuse to see the parent or follow through on visitation. They don't even want to talk on the phone. Sometimes the hostility lasts for a year or so, sometimes longer. Wasn't Dad (or Mom) responsible for breaking up your family? It's only right that you strike back and let him or her know how you feel, what they've done to you. Perhaps you believe your meanness is a way of sticking up for the parent who's been wronged, while it serves the other one right for abandoning and rejecting you.

You will eventually have to come to terms with all your anger. You only hurt yourself when you retaliate. Revenge strikes out at the other person, but it lashes back and destroys something fine in you. If both of your parents want to spend time with you, don't ignore them. Your Dad or Mom who lives alone in an apartment is very lonely. That's a radical change, hard to adjust to, and he or she misses family life. It's never easy. People don't realize what it's like until they're forced to live alone. They don't look ahead when they move out of the house in a huff. They're experiencing heartache, despondency and failure. It's really rough out there in this lonely world.

Maybe you believe they deserve it. Maybe. But maybe not! Give it another thought. Your father (or your mother) doesn't deserve your wrath. Life is already immensely difficult. Do all you can to heal the relationship. You may not feel like it, but at least you can talk it over with them. Tell them honestly how you feel. Honest communication may produce a lot of healing for both of you.

Avoid Hiding from Everyone

Don't go into your room, shut the door and keep yourself from everybody. Whenever you push your feelings underground you will become depressed and start feeling sorry for yourself. Pouting is a waste of time. Get out of that room. Start circulating. Sure, you need to give yourself private time. Some kids run much of the time and don't get in touch with themselves. They need

118

their friends around them every single moment. That may not be your problem. Your problem is the opposite —you're hiding. But that's not healthy either.

Look around you. Come out of hiding. Consider the people who need you. What you say and do may help somebody else in your family. You may be surprised how much comfort and consolation you can give that parent who lives at home. He or she really needs a lot of comfort and help. You have no idea how much! And so do your brothers or sisters. They need you, and you need them. So come out of hiding and express yourself by finding something kind to do. When you help someone else it helps you too. You benefit because you feel better.

Stop Agitating the Situation

Perhaps you're thinking to yourself: "If I stir up trouble maybe things will get better. Maybe Dad will come back home when Mom realizes she can't handle me." Only you haven't said this out loud. The words stick in your throat.

Michele caused her mother lots of trouble and herself too: "For five years I was a holy terror, not coming home on time at all. I was as obstinate as I could be. Sometimes I stayed out till three or four and once till six. Mom called the police and everything. I saw how distraught she was, and I felt terrible for a while. Then it wore off. At first I blamed her for the whole life change, being without my father, being in a new school— anything that came along I blamed her for. Even now I still have some anger."

Michele began to help herself: "I started at the new school and eventually fell into a group of kids that were most responsive to me. They were churchgoers. I totally turned away from God and church during the divorce!

I had been brought up in the Sunday School, but I refused to go when I was 13. I didn't have anything in common with church people. My parents kept going, but I put my foot down.

"In the new school I started going to socials and basketball games with church people. They all were excited about their faith and I got curious. Eventually the church became my substitute family. Christmas and Thanksgiving I spent with church people. I've done it for five years! I never understood before the intensity of the love I learned about, the love of God through these people that reached me when I most needed it. I could have gone in any direction, but church kept me from going off on the wrong track."

Don't agitate the situation. Your home is already troubled enough. Your family doesn't need any more disharmony and unpleasantness. This is the time when everyone needs some peace, even you. Whenever you throw a tantrum and cause more trouble, you are accelerating the tension. If life is already close to the edge of explosion, one more spark could set it off!

Look for Help in the Right Places

Tom is a teenage jock, blond and muscular. He found help from church friends: "Seventh and eighth grades were pretty bad. I got into trouble with the teachers. I got suspended. I got into the wrong group—kids who smoke cigarettes and all that. I used to smoke pot and Mom never knew. I went to live with my father. When he married again we got this big family. That was the rough period in the eighth grade. They forced me to go to this Christian camp and that's what got me out of the smoking and stuff. I'm glad I went. It was a lot of fun. I wasn't very active at church before. This was the first time I heard about Jesus. That changed me! Now I can't stand the smell of cigarettes or beer anymore. I'm in football and track."

Some teenagers run to other people for comfort and acceptance. That's natural. Be careful _to whom_ you run. You're vulnerable. Look for people with good morals and high standards. Look for winners. The wrong crowd very quickly influences someone who is hurting like crazy and is in a weakened condition. You may not understand it yourself. A troubled home situation may cause you to run.

Some people to whom you flee gladly accept you, because they want to introduce you to their own bad habits—smoking, alcohol, drugs. Once you start a habit it's very hard to quit. It's a lot better to never start than to have to stop! Some young people turn to sex for feeling accepted. You _are_ vulnerable. You hurt. You want to be accepted by someone. By anyone? It's not wrong to want to be accepted, but recognize the danger signals. Find a turned-on church that specializes in youth programs as Michele did. Become active in sports as Tom did. Write out your interests and goals and move in a positive direction. Help yourself to a better lifestyle.

Liz, nearly 21, looked back with lots of maturity on the divorce which had happened when she was 15. She found help eventually in professional counseling: "The last couple of years before they split, it was pretty uptight. But it never crossed my mind that my parents would divorce. This divorce really shook me up, you know. It came at a bad time. It never would have been a good time, but maybe younger I would have adjusted better. Maybe older I would have understood more. At 13 and 14 I felt that I was the ugliest person in the world, so insecure. And then to have that happen _it just kept me at that age emotionally_ until I was 20 and worked

121

through analysis. I felt emotionally stuck at 13 and 14! Analysis helped me to understand myself. I just couldn't say the word 'divorce.' The counselor made me say it over and over until I was letting the things that were inside me pour out. It was incredible. So many things I felt angry about! I just had never told anyone. Not my mother or my dad. It was destroying me."

Liz talked about helping other kids who are going through family crisis. She believes you should force your parents to help you: "Knowing what I know now, I would demand more honesty from my parents. Make them talk to you rather than you doing some juvenile act to gain their attention. At 15 you have rights too. Tell your parents that you want to know straight what is going on. (You don't have to know all the sexual problems.) Ask, 'Where do I fit in?' I never demanded that. They set themselves up as model parents. They didn't tell anything of their problems and that's not fair. But love your parents, because they're going through a lot of emotional stress."

She added a final thought carefully: "It *was* and *is* the *most traumatic thing that ever happened in my life!* It completely changed everyting—the direction I was headed. I'm really happy I managed to keep my head above it all. Before I enter into a marriage and have kids, I have to think hard—'What if this marriage ends? What will be the effect on those kids?' I probably would never have thought of that before."

Profit from the Mistakes of Others

Sometimes people say: "If parents get divorced, so will their children after they marry." The possibility exists. But we hope that life's learning experiences will give you the desire, the will and the power to succeed where your parents may have failed.

"Well, I don't plan to get married right out of school. You know, 'Okay, guys, here I am.' " Helen laughed. "I plan to get married in my twenties. I'm going to date for a while, get to know where he's coming from. Find out if we're compatible. And when we get married and have problems we'll iron them out."

"Divorce has made me more careful. I don't want someone who fits into the image of my father." commented Alice.

"I would avoid a long-distance relationship," expressed Shirley. "If I met somebody at camp from halfway across the country, I wouldn't be interested. That's how my parents met. I've thought about marriage," she added seriously. "I think you've got to marry a Christian. When I date a Christian guy I find that he is much nicer, more considerate, loving and tender. In the past the guys I dated were turkeys. With a Christian guy I have something in common. And that is the Lord."

Marge was wearing an engagement ring: "I'm really scared of marriage. After having a divorce in the family, I want my marriage to work out. I'm being careful, taking my time. Probably in a year or so we'll get married. If you don't talk to each other it's not really that good. If something bothers you and you don't say anything, it's liable to build up in you and explode. I think communication is most of it."

Sherry spoke from the backdrop of an early, threatening family life: "When I get married and have kids I'm not going to get divorced because, well, first of all I'm not going to get married unless I know it's going to last for a long, long time and I'm really sure of myself. And if I have kids I wouldn't get divorced until the kids were moved out, because I don't think it's fair for the kids to have to suffer. Unless they requested it of me and said, 'You know, it's miserable here.' One thing I'm going to make sure—no violence! I can tell just by looking at a person—by how he acts—if he is violent. They may not think it shows, but I know by the way a person is. But I have a boyfriend and he treats me good."

Melody loves life: "I don't want divorce in my life. Parents have all this pent-up stuff inside. So they take it out on the children. And the children wonder why they're being yelled at. I love life. I want a happy life. Mom says she's glad that I'm not like her. She says I'm more secure."

"When I get married it's going to work!" stated Earl emphatically. "Divorce is no option. I don't want to go through any of that."

These teenagers were forced to think through future relationships because of their family life. They might not have otherwise. The rude interruption of divorce has brought about a useful awakening, creating more sensitivity toward other people.

Suggested Reading

Ahlem, Lloyd H. *How to Cope*. Glendale, CA: Regal Books, 1978. Clear biblical insights, psychological principles and case studies on how to cope with crisis, stress and change.

Berne, Eric. *What Do You Say After You Say Hello?* New York: Grove Press, 1972. Contains insights into human behavior for the serious reader.

Berry, Jo. *Can You Love Yourself?* Glendale, CA: Regal Books, 1978. Biblical principles to help you build a strong self-image.

Despert, J. Louise. *Children of Divorce*. New York: Doubleday & Company, Inc., 1953. Describes the pitfalls of divorce and shows concern for survival of the family in America.

Dobson, James. *Dare to Discipline*. Wheaton: Tyndale House Publishers; Glendale: Regal Books, 1970. This "classic" on authoritative, but not dictatorial, child-rearing stresses importance of discipline in the parent-child relationship.

Dobson, James. *Hide or Seek*. Old Tappan, NJ: Fleming H. Revell, 1974. A thought provoking discussion of how parents (and society in general) judge and tear apart children's self-esteem. Dobson gives strategies for helping build your child's self-image. Equally helpful to parents of younger children and to parents of teenagers.

Gaulke, Earl H., *You Can Have a Family Where Everybody Wins.* St. Louis, MO: Concordia Publishing House, 1975. A Christian perspective on Parent Effectiveness Training—a course of study developed by Thomas Gordon. Gaulke establishes how Gordon's parenting principles in PET can be used with biblical doctrine and Christian love.

Grollman, Earl A., ed. *Explaining Divorce to Children.* Boston: Beacon Press, Inc. 1972. Nine experts from divergent background discuss the problem of divorce and children.

Kesler, Jay. *Too Big to Spank.* Glendale, CA: Regal Books, 1978. Ideas that make living with a teenager much easier.

McRoberts, Darlene, *Second Marriage.* Minneapolis, MN: Augsburg Publishing House, 1978. The author draws from her own experience and interviews with other remarried women and men. Especially helpful to the remarried or the person who is considering remarriage.

Osborne, Cecil G. *The Art of Understanding Your Mate.* New York: Doubleday & Company, Inc., 1970. Practical, realistic approach to marriage.

Powell, John. *Why Am I Afraid to Tell You Who I Am?* Niles, IL: Argus Communications, 1969. Deals with interpersonal relationships and emotions.

Richards, Arlene and Willis, Irene. *How to Get It Together When Your Parents Are Coming Apart.* New York: Bantam Books, Inc., 1976. Helps children and their parents learn to talk over conflicts as a step toward resolving them.

126

Richards, Lawrence O., *You, the Parent.* Chicago, IL: Moody Press, 1974. Richards discusses practicing communication through love, family unity, good discipline, parental authority and family worship experiences. Parents are given help in how to become aware of the child's character growth and spiritual needs.

Skoglund, Elizabeth. *Can I Talk to You?* Glendale, CA: Regal Books, 1977. Suggestions for parents, teachers and church leaders in guiding young people in their problems of today.

Small, Dwight, *Divorce.* Glendale, CA: Regal Books, 1977. A 40-page question and answer book that grapples with problems like: emotional struggles the divorced person faces; divorce's effect on self-image; coming to grips with pre-divorce events; encouragement the divorced person wants and needs. Answers based on biblical principles along with study/discussion ideas add to the value and practicality of this compact book.

Smoke, Jim, *Growing Through Divorce.* Irving, CA: Harvest House Publishers, 1976. Practical guidelines for facing the changes associated with divorce, accepting new roles, responsibilities and relationships, single-parenting, weekend parenting, stepparenting.

Wakefield, Norm, *You Can Have a Happier Family.* Glendale, CA: Regal Books, 1977. Wakefield discusses four goals based on biblical principles for developing a Christian family life-style. An enthusiastic father of five, the author encourages parents with practical ways how they can achieve these goals.

Wise, Robert L. *When There Is No Miracle.* Glendale, CA: Regal Books, 1977. Grapples realistically and biblically with the unanswerable mysteries and questions that face us all.